I0087540

SCI-FI Fantasy Baby Names for the TWENTY-FIRST CENTURY

SCI-FI Fantasy Baby Names for the TWENTY-FIRST CENTURY

Anime, Authors, Actors, Dark Lords, Disney Princesses, Myth, Magic, Mayhem, Superheroes, Scientists, and Everything Else

Valerie Estelle Frankel

Other Works by Valerie Estelle Frankel

Henry Potty and the Pet Rock: A Harry Potter Parody
Henry Potty and the Deathly Paper Shortage: A Harry Potter Parody
Buffy and the Heroine's Journey
From Girl to Goddess: The Heroine's Journey in Myth and Legend
Katniss the Cattail: The Unauthorized Guide to Name and Symbols
The Many Faces of Katniss Everdeen: The Heroine of The Hunger Games
Harry Potter, Still Recruiting: A Look at Harry Potter Fandom
Teaching with Harry Potter
An Unexpected Parody: The Spoof of The Hobbit Movie
Teaching with Harry Potter
Myths and Motifs in The Mortal Instruments
Winning the Game of Thrones: The Host of Characters & their Agendas
Winter is Coming: Symbols, Portents, and Hidden Meanings in A Game of Thrones
Bloodsuckers on the Bayou: The Myths, Symbols, and Tales Behind HBO's True Blood
The Girl's Guide to the Heroine's Journey
Choosing to be Insurgent or Allegiant: Symbols, Themes & Analysis of the Divergent Trilogy
Doctor Who and the Hero's Journey: The Doctor and Companions as Chosen Ones
Doctor Who: The What Where and How
Sherlock: Every Canon Reference You May Have Missed in BBC's Series
Symbols in Game of Thrones
How Game of Thrones Will End
Joss Whedon's Names
Pop Culture in the Whedonverse
Women in Game of Thrones: Power, Conformity, and Resistance
History, Homages and the Highlands: An Outlander Guide
The Catch-Up Guide to Doctor Who
Remember All Their Faces: A Deeper Look at Character, Gender and the Prison World of Orange Is The New Black
Everything I Learned in Life I Know from Joss Whedon
Empowered: The Symbolism, Feminism, and Superheroism of Wonder Woman
The Avengers Face their Dark Sides
The Comics of Joss Whedon: Critical Essays
Mythology in Game of Thrones

To Beatrice Michaela, Bennett Raphael, and the new little Alexandra Rose – sweet tiny cousins with perfectly normal names.

With thanks to Steve Frankel, Steve Ginzburg, Daniel Lowd, J. Malcolm Stewart, and the Whensday Group for their hilarious advice.

This book is an unauthorized guide and commentary on many series. None of the individuals or companies associated with the comics, television show, films, books, etc., mentioned here have in any way sponsored, approved, endorsed, or authorized this book.

ISBN-13: 978-0692587362 (LitCrit Press)
ISBN-10: 0692587365

Introduction

A science fiction baby name guide is an invaluable resource. Think of all the people groping for inspiration who might otherwise not have considered Neelix. Or Darth. Or Medusa. To these people wise enough to *not* consider painful baby names, this guide offers a quick look at what you've missed, and hopefully a giggle. How popular are *Game of Thrones* names today, or Disney ones, or names from *Buffy*? This guide endeavors to answer those questions.

But let's say your spouse, perhaps even (gasp) a nongeek, is eager for a name like Jennifer. After looking it up in this guide, you can pride yourself on your potential child sharing a name with two women of *Star Trek*, a *Buffy* heroine, a cross-dressing lesbian from *Doctor Who*, a Gelfling and a She-Hulk. It seems essential to have this list before so-naming your child then parading her around the convention circuit before she can talk (perhaps her first word will be grok!)

Included is a long list of conventional and unconventional American names, with some rather ridiculous sf ones mixed in. Some are ranked on a scale from five happy babies to five sad babies, in this author's opinion, of course. All are defined, with their science fiction-fantasy references, and some have statistics on their popularity, as Khaleesi and Elsa soar. Some are ridiculous and others are just painful.

Fairly or not, most classic American baby names derive from Western Europe or *their* sources – Greece, Rome, and the Bible. A few of the more particularly Welsh or German names may sound strange to us (Brunhilda, anyone?) but many like Randolph and Alberich form the Randy and Albert of modern times.

Thus the collection centers around names of American/European origins.

Perhaps fans would like an Indian or Chinese geek name? These, along with Arabic, Spanish, Russian, and African ones, plus Japanese anime/manga names appear in their own separate section. They were mostly named by authors seeking classical ethnic names to show multiculturalism in the *X-Men* or *Ender's Game,* for instance. Of course, there are also international scientists, inventors, and astronauts. So if you're considering Suki or Sandeep, that's where to look. Now let's begin…

Names A-Z

Aaron, a priestly name from the Bible, is surprisingly unpopular in sf and f. Aaron Douglas plays Chief Galen Tyrol on new *Battlestar Galactica,* while Aron Eisenberg plays Rom on *DS9.*

Aahz, a green, scaly "demon" (short for "dimension traveler") comes from the dimension of Perv from *Myth Adventures.* You want a Perv named Aahz?

Aberforth Dumbledore is Albus Dumbledore's brother, owner of the Hog's Head. No idea what his name means or why you'd inflict it on a kid.

In the Biblical story of King David, Abigail brings supplies to David, deterring him from killing her husband. Abigail Brand of Whedon's newly created Marvel's S.W.O.R.D. (Sentient World Observation and Response Department) is much more aggressive. She's joined by Abigail "Abby" Mills, from the TV show *Sleepy Hollow.* Other Abigails are the daughter of King Midas in *Once Upon a Time* and the forensic specialist on *NCIS*. "Abigail" means "my father is joyful." #12 in 2015.

In Hebrew Abraham means "Father of a multitude," as the Old Testament patriarch Abram changed his name to this. Bram Stoker was the author of *Dracula.* There's an Abe in the game *Oddworld.* Also Grandpa Simpson.

Acheron Hades is the criminal mastermind in the *Thursday Next* series. The River Acheron is one of the rivers of Hell, so possibly a problem for bouncing babies. Not that the book character's much better.

Achilles was the most badass warrior of all time, who chose a short and glorious life in the Trojan War and died there. This name also goes to a villain in the *Ender's Game* series, though his is pronounced as the French A-shille. Be warned – achos is Greek for pain, which is what you'll find if you name your kid for a big fighter.

Augusta Ada King, Countess of Lovelace, helped program the Babbage Engine, inventing the first machine algorithm. It's from the Germanic for "noble" and an excellent name for your boundary-breaking baby. Of course, this was also the creepy but brave and assertive Victorian of *Doctor Who*'s "The Crimson Horror."

Adam: There are many Adams in science fiction. The name means man, and such a primal character is easily found on many alien worlds. Prince Adam is He-Man's secret identity in *Masters of the Universe.* Adam is a Frankenstein character on *Buffy,* and in fact the original name Mary Shelley chose for Frankenstein's monster. Adam Mitchell was briefly a companion to the Ninth Doctor and Rose of *Doctor Who.* DC superhero Adam Strange and Marvel superhero Adam Warlock suggest a similar wavelength. Adam Park is a Mighty Morphin Power Ranger. Adam Eddington is a romantic interest in some of Madeleine L'Engle's books and Adam Young stars in *Good Omens.* Adam and Lilith Clay are the parents of the superheroine in *Girl Genius. The Secret Circle* has another. Actors include Adam Baldwin (Jayne from *Firefly*). Adama, clearly named for first man Adam, is the hero on *Battlestar Galactica.* It's a good name – so say we all!

Adara ("virgin" or "noble") shares its name with Adhara, one of the brightest stars in the sky. Adara is a heroine in *The Belgariad* and the embodiment of hope in *Green Lantern* comics. Shining and lovely.

Adele and its many variants mean noble. Adele Stackhouse is Sookie's beloved grandmother on *True Blood*, while Adie is a heroine in *The Sword of Truth*. Both delightful but elderly mentors to the younger characters. As a variant, Adilyn Braelyn Charlaine Danika Bellefleur is a part-fairy on *True Blood*. Science fiction author Aldous Huxley, who wrote *Brave New World*, has a similar name. Perhaps the British R&B and soul singer of the same name has a super power for Record Sales?

Young Adric delighted many as boy genius and *Doctor Who* companion. Still, he has an indelible connection with the name, unless its new bearer chooses to be a wizard.

Adrian Tchaikovsky is a British fantasy and science fiction author. Vigilante (Adrian Chase) is a hero of *New Teen Titans*. The name means "sea."

Æon Flux stars in her own action movie, with a name that means life or timeless. It's a superhero name, though rather ridiculous. And possibly how long it may take her to get over this early childhood blow.

Samuel L. Jackson voiced the character Afro Samurai – a butt kicker. As the first black male title character in an anime, his name's a bit too obvious (but the Afro was indeed, so excellent).

Agatha, meaning "good," is ironically the mean headmistress of Crunchem Hall in Roald Dahl's *Matilda*. She's also the spunky inventor heroine of the *Girl Genius* comic books and a *Pokémon* character. In *Minority Report*, one of the Precogs by this name has deviant visions of the future. The mystery writer Agatha Christie can be added to the list. As a variant, Agda and Mella are Golgafrinchan girls that Arthur and Ford hit on in *Hitchhiker's Guide*.

Agnes (Greek for pure) appears in *Despicable Me*, while Agnes Robertson Arber was the first woman botanist and the third overall to have been elected as a Fellow of the Royal Society. Agnes Nutter is a seer with a reputation as, you guessed it, in *Good Omens*.

Agrajag is a piteous creature that is continually reincarnated and subsequently killed, each time unknowingly, by Arthur Dent in *Hitchhiker's Guide*. Don't thrust this fate on the kid.

Ahsoka from *Star Wars* has a fascinating name. It does sound like Aw, sucker, though.

Aiden characters star in *Teen Wolf* and *Being Human* US, and one is also a warrior in *The Elder Scrolls*. More fictional characters include one from the book *The Secret of Kells*, while Aidan Lynch appears in *Harry Potter and the Goblet of Fire*. From the old Irish name Áedán, this is the name of an Irish monk and several characters in Irish mythology. It comes from the old Irish Áed, "fire," a fantasy name in itself. Hugh is a variant. Five normal babies – this name's been quite popular lately – #9.

Alan/Alanna/Alayne and its many variants mean "little rock" or "handsome" in Breton. Tamora Pierce wrote a series of middle grade fantasies on Alanna, the hero who disguises herself and becomes a knight and her trickster-spy daughter Aly (Alianne). Alan Shepard, the first American in space, flew on Mercury-Redstone 3 and Apollo 14. Alan Bean, who walked on the moon, was an astronaut on Apollo 12 and Skylab 3. Alan Turing was a pioneer in artificial intelligence during World War II.

In fantasy, Alan Alexander Milne was the author of the *Winnie the Pooh* books. Allan Quatermain was a hero in *The League of Extraordinary Gentlemen*. Allen Francis Doyle was a guardian angel character on *Angel.* Alan Scott was the first Green Lantern, while Alan Bradley stars in *Tron.*

Alan Tudyk is the actor who played Wash on *Firefly*. American screenwriter and producer Alan Ball created *True Blood.* Alan Cumming, the actor, was in *X-Men 2, Riverworld, Goldeneye, Spy Kids,* and many more films. There's science fiction author Alan Dean Foster and comic book creator Alan Moore. Alan Sidney Patrick Rickman played Snape in all the *Harry Potter*s, the Sherriff in *Robin Hood: Prince of Thieves,* Marvin in *Hitchhiker's Guide,* the Caterpillar in Disney's live action *Alice in Wonderland,* and countless other roles.

For variants, Allayne is the last name of *Firefly*'s warrior woman Zoe. Sansa calls herself Alayne while disguised in the *Game of Thrones* books. Alianora is the clever princess of Duchy of Toure-on-Marsh in Patricia C. Wrede's *Enchanted Forest Chronicles.* Five normal babies plus a bonus point for getting so many scifi-fantasy characters. Just beware of Alianora, even if it does contain the word "alien."

Alaric Saltzman of *The Vampire Diaries* has a wizardly name for "noble," shared with a character in Stephen King's *The Dark Tower* series.

Alastair: An excellent wizard name, Scottish variant on Alexander, meaning "defending man." Alastor "Mad-Eye" Moody is a *Harry Potter* Auror and member of the Order of the Phoenix. It's classy and striking but hardly usual.

Alberich is the dwarf of the Norse ring cycle and an honorable warrior in Mercedes Lackey's *Valdemar* books. The wizardly name comes from Germanic elements alf "elf" and ric "power." Possibly you're naming for your German ancestors, otherwise this seems like a heavy operatic burden. Two sad babies.

Albert Einstein lends distinction to "Albert," Germanic for noble and bright. In addition, Albert Abraham Michelson was the first American to be awarded a Nobel Prize in Physics while Alby stars in *The Maze Runner*. Rear Admiral Albert Calavicci is Sam's hologram advisor on *Quantum Leap*. Five normal babies.

Albus Dumbledore, Hogwarts Headmaster, has a Latin name that means "white." *Harry Potter*'s huge legacy puts this at one sad baby.

Alcide Herveaux is a romantic lead on *True Blood* – one of the many werewolves who look hot with their shirts off. Alcide is the French/Italian variant of "Alcides," another name for Heracles. This name was used for several operas on the subject. One normal baby, since naming for the brawling Greek hero or the shirtless werewolf seems suspect.

Aldur is the all-powerful god of *The Belgariad* by David Eddings. Alder, for the tree, is a *Pokémon* character. Despite this, it seems obscure enough to rate only one normal baby.

Alecto: Alecto Carrow is a Death Eater and evil professor of Muggle Studies in the final *Harry Potter* books; she takes her name from one of the Furies of Greek myth. Three sad babies for naming after an underworld shrew, though admittedly this is a rather obscure reference.

Alexander was #14 in 2015. This famous name, "defending men," has many bearers in fantasy from Alex Murphy (Robocop) to infamous Lex Luthor. All of course take their names from Alexander the Great. It's the name of the X-Men Hero Havok (Alexander Summers), loveable *Buffy* sidekick Xander Harris, and a hero of the *King's Quest* computer games. In *Star Trek,* Alexander

Siddig plays Doctor Bashir, and Worf's son is another Alexander. Alex Murphy is Robocop, while Alec Holland is the alter-ego of Swamp Thing. Dr. Alexis Zarkov stars in *Flash Gordon.* Alex Burgess keeps Dream imprisoned in Neil Gaiman's *The Sandman.* His name almost certainly derives from Anthony Burgess's *A Clockwork Orange* – where the main character is Alex. Alexander Murray is the father in *A Wrinkle in Time,* and his son, Sandy, is one of the "normal" kids in their sciency family. Lisa Milbrand wrote in *Parents Magazine* that Xander clearly got a boost from its pop culture association – it didn't even register on the charts when Buffy first aired, and it's now nearing the top 200 names.

In real life, the name has been used by kings of Scotland, Poland and Yugoslavia, emperors of Russia, and eight popes. In science, it includes Scottish-Canadian explorer Sir Alexander MacKenzie and Alexander Graham Bell, inventor of the telephone. Alexander Firming discovered penicillin. Variants include Alec: Alec Guinness played the original Obi-Wan, while Alec Lightwood is a teen demon hunter in *The Mortal Instruments.* Alek stars in *The Nine Lives of Chloe King.* Alessandro Juliani plays Lt. Gaeta on new *Battlestar Galactica.* Alexis Rogers is the spunky daughter on *Castle,* while Alexis Denisof plays a heroic demon hunter on *Angel.* Whoppi Goldberg's daughter is Alexandrea. Alexa Canady was the first black female neurosurgeon and another Alexa was a character on *Highlander.* Five normal babies.

Alfred is an Old English name. Since it means elf-counselor, it's very fantastical already, though it certainly masquerades as normal. Dr. Alfred Prunesquallor appears in *Gormenghast.* Alfred Bester wrote science fiction classics such as *The Stars My Destination.* Science fiction characters on *Babylon 5* and *Firefly* were named for him. Alfred Wegener proposed the theory of continental drift and

Alfred Russel Wallace discovered the concept of evolution by natural selection. Alfred M. Worden was Command Module Pilot on Apollo 15. British poet Alfred Lord Tennyson adds distinction, as does Alfred Nobel and any name that's followed by "the Great." And there's always the alien ALF. There's the Atom from the comics (Al Pratt) and Sam's friend Al Calavicci in *Quantum Leap*. Avery Brooks (Captain Sisko on DS9) has a variant, as does Captain Avery of *Doctor Who*'s "The Curse of the Black Spot." However, in the superhero world, minds will instantly drift to Batman's all-too-proper butler. Four normal babies, minus one for the counseling elves and brooding superheroes thing.

Algernon Rowan-Webb is a character on *The Worst Witch*. French for "moustached man." *Flowers for Algernon* makes this a nice scifi namesake, if your child is a smart little mouse.

Alice, a Celtic baby name meaning Noble, is related to Adele. The obvious character is of course Alice in Wonderland – even minds that aren't sci-fi oriented will go there straightaway. On the other hand, this Alice was the original girl power heroine, generations before Hermione Granger. Speaking of Harry Potter, Alice Longbottom is Neville's mother, driven mad, while

Alyssa Milano played one of the main character sisters on *Charmed*. Alicia Spinnet is Chaser on the Gryffindor Quidditch team. Alice Abernathy, heroine from the *Resident Evil* film series, is named for the Wonderland girl of course. For other namesakes, Alice Cullen is the smart, future-reading vampire of *Twilight*. Black Alice, real name Lori Zechlin, is a DC Comics character introduced in *Birds of Prey*. Actresses include *Smallville*'s Allison Mack (Chloe Sullivan) and *Buffy*'s Willow – Alyson Hannigan. Finally, just to distinguish the name further, Alice Mary Norton is the real name of science fiction author Andre Norton, and

Alice Bradley Sheldon wrote as James Tiptree, Jr., both hiding their genders so they could be published. Alice Guy-Blaché was the first woman to own a production studio. Alice is also a programming language. It's also worth noting that Alice Beeblebrox is Zaphod's favorite mother in *Hitchhiker's Guide.*

In a French variant, Alais de la Courcel is a clever princess in the Kushiel series by Jacqueline Carey. Alison Blaire is Dazzler of the X-Men, while Allison stars in *Teen Wolf.* Alyssa Ogawa is the competent nurse on *Star Trek: TNG* and Alynna Nechayev is the visiting tough-as-nails admiral. Four normal babies, minus one for the *Alice in Wonderland* jokes she'll be stuck with.

Allanon, Merlin-like wizard of *The Sword of Shannara,* has a name that unfortunately sounds like Al-anon. Better not foresee *this* future.

The most obvious "Alma" is the Battle of Alma, the first battle of the Crimean War. British Almas all take their names from here, including the cruel leader of The Hunger Games. Alma also means "nourishing" or "guiding spirit" in Latin, creating the phrase "Alma mater," or nourishing mother. Three normal babies – it's an unusual name coming from a violent battle and a violent fictional leader. But it rose 175 spots after 2012.

Almalexia is an immortal in *The Elder Scrolls.* This seems to combine Alma with Lexia, the written word. Three sad babies – can you imagine how long it'll be before she can pronounce her own name?

Forbidden Planet offers Altaira "What's a swimsuit" Morbius. Despite this, the name is particularly scifi since it's Greek for star.

There have been many vampires in anime, but none

have been as nasty as Alucard, a deliciously sadistic vampire from the anime *Hellsing*, (and also a transposition of Bad Vlad's title), who loves to torture monsters. Well, someone has to.

Alvin is the boy hero of Orson Scott Card's Alvin Maker series, while Alvin Kersh is an FBI character from *The X-Files.* Despite this and its German meaning of "noble friend," the name seems permanently associated with the chipmunk. Four normal babies and one rodent.

Amalthea is the human alias of *The Last Unicorn.* It was also the magic goat that fed Zeus. Memorable in a stand-out sort of way. Two sad babies, or three if you tell the kid you named her for an *actual* kid.

Amanda: There's one in Nikita, while Amanda Grayson is the human mother of Spock and also Zoe's mother on *Caprica*.. The name means beloved. Five normal babies, plus a bonus for a secret science-fiction connection few will pick up on.

Amber means the stone of course. *The Chronicles of Amber* is a beloved series of fantasy novels by Roger Zelazny. There's Amberle, princess of Shannara and butt-kicking chosen one. Also, Amber Benson played the beloved witch Tara on *Buffy*. Four normal babies, since anything based on an English word is a bit wobbly. To say nothing of naming after a mystical fantasy kingdom.

Early science fiction writer Ambrose Bierce is derived from the element "ambrosios," meaning immortal, divine. Ambrosius (Latin) was borne by the 5th-centur British leader Ambrosius Aurelianus, the historical basis for the legendary King Arthur himself.

Amethyst, Princess of Gemworld shares her name

with Amethyst, heroine of *The Ordinary Princess.* Name comes with obligatory winged horse and crown. Good for princess fans, likely bad for fitting in at school, though Amy is always an option. Two sad babies.

Amelia means "work." Amelia Earhart, the famed American aviator, gives this name historical glory, though science fiction fans will associate it with *Doctor Who* companion Amelia Pond.

Amy main characters appear in *The Big Bang Theory,* and *Futurama,* while Amy Madison is a witch in *Buffy* (known for several seasons as Amy the Rat). Amelia Bones is Head of the Department of Magical Law Enforcement in *Harry Potter.* Amelia Wil Tesla Saillune stars in the anime *Slayers.* For princess fans, Amelia "Mia" Thermopolis is the title character of *The Princess Diaries.* Namesakes appear in *The Aristocats, Touch,* and *Underworld*, with more in the children's TV series *The Worst Witch* and the *Rainbow Magic* book series. Amy Briggs created *Plundered Hearts,* the first computer game for girls. There's also Amelia Bloomer and Amelia Bedelia. But beware! Amelia Sackville-Baggins is an annoying Hobbit character. Five normal babies for Amy or Amelia. In fact, Oliver and Amelia were top 2014 names (Williams)

"She's beauty, she's grace, she'll punch you in the face." America Chavez is the superheroine Miss America. Another America is the star of the dystopian teen series *The Selection.*

Amidala from *Star Wars* (Italian for beautiful flower) could arguably relate to Amelia, and such a child could certainly be called Amy. She'll likely insist on it. Three sad babies.

Amos means "carried" in Hebrew, a prophet of the Old Testament. Amos Diggory, Cedric's father, works for the Department for the Regulation and Control of Magical Creatures in the *Harry Potter* series. Phillip J. Fry of *Futurama* has an ancestor of this name. Two sad babies for being rather old fashioned and not terribly science-fictional.

Amycus is the name of a son of Poseidon. Though it means "friendly," it's the name of brutal Amycus Carrow in *Harry Potter*, professor of Dark Arts. Three sad babies for the *Harry Potter* thing and the strangeness. Couldn't you just call the kid Harry? Or in this case, Spawn of Satan?

Anafiel Delaunay de Montrève is a spymaster hero in the *Kushiel* series by Jacqueline Carey. His is an angel's name, meaning "He who sees God." Seems a bit much for a helpless baby. Three sad babies.

Over 200 boys were named Anakin in 2014 (Holeman). But who does that? Anakin becomes evil and everyone knows it. Resist the dark side of naming! Resist!

Anastasia means "resurrection," the Russian feminine form of the Greek male name Anastasios (popular for its saintly connections). Anastasia Dualla is a beloved character on *Battlestar Galactica,* while Anastasia and Drizella are Cinderella's stepsisters in the Disney version. Also, *Anastasia* is a beloved cartoon movie, starring the lost daughter of the Romanovs who's likely the most famous holder of this name. It can be shortened to Stacy.

Andrew, meaning manly or brave, has its science fiction characters. Central must be the real name of Ender, from *Ender's Game.* Still, actors Andrew Robinson (Garek of *Star Trek: DS9*) and Andy Serkis (Gollum) must join the list. Andrew Wells is the geek on *Buffy*, who begins as an amoral villain but slowly gains responsibility. Altogether

Andrews is a homeless, mad character in Terry Pratchett's *Discworld*, while Andy Bellefleur is a hapless character on *True Blood.* Andy is also the kid of *Toy Story* and Prue's first love on *Charmed.* The feminine flip is Andrea of course. The French would be Andre, as in Andre Norton. Since this author was actually female, you might want to name for her real name, Alice. Andrew is patron saint of Scotland and Russia, and one of the apostles. Five normal babies for Andrew or Andrea. Also, Drew is a character in *Percy Jackson,* and Drew Fuller plays Chris Halliwell, the second son of Leo and Piper on *Charmed.*

Andromeda is the heroine of the myth Perseus and also the ship (though with a human actress) in the science fiction series of that name. Another is a ship in *Percy Jackson.* Also, Andromeda Tonks is grandmother of Teddy Remus Lupin in Harry Potter. Strangely it means "to think of a man" from the Greek. Two sad babies – you can shorten it, but it's pretty mythological. And naming after the wimpy bound princess obsessed (apparently) with thinking of men might earn you that elusive third baby.

Angel/Angela obviously means angel. Angela, a comic book character created by Neil Gaiman, appears in the "Age of Ultron" storyline and in *Guardians of the Galaxy.* More characters include Angela Petrelli (*Heroes*), Angelica Teach (Blackbeard's daughter from *Pirates of the Caribbean: On Stranger Tides*), Angela Del Toro (Marvel superhero White Tiger), and Angela from the anime and manga series *Soul Eater.* Angelina Johnson is a Gryffindor student two years above Harry Potter, Quidditch Chaser and captain. Angelica Jones is Firestar (X-Men), while another Angelica was Bilbo's niece. Angelie is a heroine in *The Elder Scrolls,* Angeline Fowl is Artemis Fowl's mother, and Angeline is Jaenelle's last name in *The Black Jewels Trilogy.* Queen Angella appears on *Princess of Power.*

Actors include Angelina Jolie (Lara Croft) and

Angelica Houston (*The Witches, Ever After, The Mists of Avalon*). Meanwhile, British author Angela Carter wrote *Shadow Dance* and many beloved fairytale adaptations. Angel Coulby plays Guinevere on *Merlin.* Four normal babies.

Anne/Anna is a very popular name, from the Hebrew for grace or favor. The *Buffy* series has many including Anne Pratt (Spike's mother), Anya Jenkins, Anne Steele, Anaheed (in the comics) and of course Buffy Anne Summers, likely named for X-Men's spunky Kitty Anne Pryde. Other X-Men include Anna Marie Darkholme, Rogue, who was played by Anna Paquin in the films. (Paquin also plays Sookie Stackhouse on *True Blood).*

Babylon 5's captain has a shock when his wife Anna Sheridan arrives back from the dead – and evil. Sweet Annie Cresta is Katniss's friend in *Mockingjay,* and there's an Annie in *Being Human UK.*

While the name Elsa skyrocketed after *Frozen*, Elsa's sister, Anna, didn't get much of a bump, rising only one spot in the rankings just after the film's release to become the 34th most common girl's name (Wolfers). Authors include Anne McCaffrey (*Dragonriders of Pern*) and Anne Rice, author of *The Vampire Chronicles.* Real life Anna Lee Fisher, M.D. was an astronaut on STS-51-A. Ann is one of the best friends in *A Great and Terrible Beauty.* There's beloved children's heroines Anne of Green Gables and Raggedy Ann.

Variants include Annabeth (Percy Jackson) Annalee (*Alien: Resurrection*), Anya or Anyanka (*Buffy* or *Soul Eater*) and Annika (Seven of Nine's real name). Anya Corazon is Spider-Girl. Lisa Milbrand wrote in *Parents Magazine* that Anya "zoomed up the charts after the character was introduced in the show [*Buffy*], and it's currently in the top 400 names." There's Anita Dearly the wife in *101 Dalmatians,* and *Anita Blake: Vampire Hunter.* Annabel was immortalized by Poe. Annette O'Toole starred in *Superman*

III. Annika is Pippi Longstocking's friend. It is also often paired with other names like Maryanne, or Joanne. Five normal babies, with bonus points for slipping in Buffy, Kitty, *Frozen* girl, and an astronaut.

Anthony, "praiseworthy," deserves a place in science fiction just for wisecracking Tony Stark. Of course, Anthony Stewart Head, who starred in *The Rocky Horror Picture Show, Merlin,* and *Buffy,* deserves honors as well. The name goes to several minor characters: Anthony Goldstein is a rather forgettable Ravenclaw student, while Antonin Dolohov is a wicked Death Eater. Anthony Montgomery plays Travis Mayweather on Stargate: Atlantis, while Antoine "Trip" Triplett who a hero on *Agents of S.H.I.E.L.D.* Anton comes from *Ratatouille.* Tony Lewis appears in the fairytale film *The 10th Kingdom.* If you're seeking strange variants, Antioch Peverell was the original owner of the Elder Wand in *Harry Potter*, while Antorell is a cruel and inept wizard in Patricia C. Wrede's *Enchanted Forest Chronicles.* Prince Thun, leader of the Lion Men in *Flash Gordon,* has a name that appears related. Don't seek strange variants. Anthony itself it a tad unusual, so four happy babies.

Apollo is a hero on *Battlestar Galactica,* obviously named for the Greek sun god. Your kid will be hot but ridiculed.

April O'Neill gets to hang with the Ninja Turtles, while bratty April Lou is Tinkerballa on *The Guild.*

Arabella Figg is the Squib neighbor of the Dursleys and member of the Order of the Phoenix. Even with no powers, she's a hero. It's German for "eagle heroine" or Latin for "yielding to prayer."

Arachne is the spider goddess of Greek myth. Several

characters are named for her in myth-related stories like the *Percy Jackson* books, comic books, and the anime and manga series *Soul Eater.* Three sad babies – it's mythic but goes to a bad lady.

Aragorn: Everyone knows this is straight from *Lord of the Rings,* and it's no longer trendy and rebellious to name your seventies kid for the series. Four sad babies, since almost no one in the world won't get this reference.

Archibald is an old guy name from the start. Archie is a bit better, but do you really want to tell the kid his birth certificate says "bald"? Archimedes is likely as bad, whether naming for the greatest scientist of the classical age – mathematician, physicist, astronomer, engineer, inventor, and weapons-designer – or the cartoon owl from *The Sword in the Stone.* Namesakes include Archie Hopper, the real identity of Jiminy Cricket in *Once Upon a Time,* or Archie the comic book character (or *Pokémon* character).

Princess Ardala stars in *Buck Rogers.* The name is Irish for high honor. Could be worse…

Argus is a disfigured monster covered in eyeballs from Greek myth, or a nasty-minded old caretaker in *Harry Potter.* A thug in both realities. Two sad babies.

Ariadne, "holy," is a heroine of Greek myth (though abandoned by the hero Theseus and often portrayed in over-revealing Creten wear). Another is in *Inception.* As varients, Ariana Dumbledore was Albus Dumbledore's little sister, while another starred in *Jurassic Park.*

Ariel is an angel name meaning "lion of God" in Hebrew, more popular as a boy's name (especially with this spelling) before *The Little Mermaid.* Ariel "Ari" Gold is a character in the HBO series *Entourage* and of course,

Ariel is the magical sprite in Shakespeare's *The Tempest.* An Ariel is the moon of Uranus and another is one of Kitty Pryde's superhero names. In Peter David's *Supergirl* run and on *Earth: Final Conflict*, superior beings have a daughter who's named this.

Ariel's sisters are Aquata, Andrina, Arista, Atina, Adella, and Alanna. All admirable.

Arlene Fowler Bellefleur is a hapless character on *True Blood.* Her name is actually a variant of Charles, "manly."

Armand is a vampire in Anne Rice's *The Vampire Chronicles*, while Armando Muñoz is Darwin of the X-Men. There's an Armin in *Shingeki no Kyojin*, while Armin Shimerman played Quark on *Star Trek: DS9* and the principal on *Buffy*.

Arnold characters are hard to take seriously, as they include the anal and unlikeable Arnold Rimmer off *Red Dwarf* and the homeless, mad Arnold Sideways in Terry Pratchett's *Discworld.* This comes from a Germanic name meaning "eagle power," but its bearers are less than heroic. Nonetheless, Arnold Sommerfeld was a pioneer of quantum and atomic physics.

Artemis is the Greek goddess of the hunt, now lending her name to the male children's book star Artemis Fowl. Another is a talking cat in *Sailor Moon.* There's secret agent Artemus Gordon of *The Wild Wild West* (original and Will Smith film). Three sad babies. Can you imagine the kid introducing himself: "Yes, I know there's a Greek goddess. Wow, no one's ever told me that…"

King Arthur is the ultimate namesake – hey, *King Arthur* is the original fantasy epic, with hundreds of knockoffs, adaptations, and homages. They likely include

Harry Potter's Arthur Weasley – father of Ron and his siblings. Arthur Curry – Aquaman may join the list. It could be derived from the Celtic elements *artos* "bear" combined with *viros* "man" or *rigos* "king" or from the Roman clan name Artorius, meaning noble, courageous.

One of the other most popular series of all time is *Sherlock Holmes,* written by Arthur Conan Doyle for another namesake. With Arthur Dent of *Hitchhiker's Guide* here and Eric Arthur Blair (George Orwell's real name) it is quite prestigious. Adding that Sir Arthur Eddington is widely considered one of the greatest astronomers of all time is only icing on the birthday cake. Four happy babies, for the King Arthur jokes.

Arwen is Welsh for "noble maiden." See everything said about Aragorn and how we needn't name for *Lord of the Rings* now that the seventies are over. Three sad babies.

Arya, "noble," was actually a name before *Game of Thrones.* Beyond Arya Stark, Arya Dröttningu is a female elf in the *Inheritance Cycle* and the love-interest of Eragon. Aria is the heroine from the anime *Aria* or in *Under the Never Sky.* It was the fastest-growing American name in 2012, and 244 Aryas were born in 2014, presumably for *Thrones* (Williams). Aria's also gaining popularity.

Aseed: Leader of the cheese-worshipping Tyromancers on the planet Nano in *Hitchhiker's Guide.* Three sad babies. Well, no one's gonna get this reference. But is that really the goal to inflict on the kid?

Asher meaning "happy" or "blessed" was one of the twelve tribes in the Old Testament, one of the less-interesting sons of Jacob, though the name is in use. Asherah was a Sumerian mother goddess. Asher is a vampire character in the *Anita Blake* books or Jonas's friend in *The Giver.*

Ashley Boyd is Cinderella in *Once Upon a Time.* This unisex name for "from the ash tree meadow" appears in *Gone with the Wind* and Hemmingway. Ash stars in *Pokémon*, of course.

Aslan. You want to name your baby for a mythical lion and Jesus analogy from Narnia? Not much else I can say really. Though the sad babies could say it for me. Perhaps Arslan, a character in *The Elder Scrolls,* is a relative.

Asriel, "help of God," or possibly "God has bound/imprisoned me" is an angel name and also the pompous villain of the *Golden Compass* series. Azrael was an angel who is said to herald the coming of the Apocalypse. He also was the angel who, at time of death, severs the soul from the body. Surely, even if the kid is supposed to help God, there are better options.

Astra means star – certainly appropriate for the science fiction lover. This is a DC comic book character and Princess Astra on *Doctor Who.* Trillian Astra stars in *The Hitchhiker's Guide to the Galaxy.* Two Astras appear in the *X-men* comics. There's another in the Japanese TV show *Ultraman Leo.*

Astrid is also "star." Astrid Lindgren is the beloved author of *Pippi Longstocking,* while Astrid Farnsworth is a character on *Fringe.* Astrid Peth was a short-lived *Doctor Who* companion. More Astrids appear in *How to Train Your Dragon* and *Once Upon a Time.*

Athena, named for the Greek goddess of wisdom, is also a (Cylon) heroine on *Battlestar Galactica.*

Atreyu is a progratonist of *The Neverending Story.* Suitable if you want a green-skinned boy (in the book anyway) who hunts the purple buffalo.

Audrey ("noble strength") is an evil alien carnivorous plant monster. Or a pair of lovely actresses. Go figure. In either case, "feed me" seems to apply.

Augusta/Augustus is the Latin for great, used by Caesar Augustus of course. Augusta "Ada" Lovelace was arguably the first programmer. August Booth is Pinocchio in *Once Upon a Time* and Augustus Gloop is the greedy kid in *Charlie and the Chocolate Factory,* though he seems the most atrocious kid in the world to name after. Another August is the villain in *Avengers* (the Steed and Peel one). Augusta Longbottom is grandmother of Neville Longbottom and a tough old lady. Augustus Rookwood is a Death Eater – Harry Potter does like those Latin names. Aughra is the Keeper of Secrets from *The Dark Crystal.* But be wary – they're rather out of fashion. Still it's great to be called "great." Two happy babies and a bouncy Oompa-loompa tune.

Aurora: Disney princess Sleeping Beauty is named for the radiant Aurora, also associated with the scientific term for the Northern Lights Ororo, the real name of X-Man Storm is likely related. Likewise, Princess Aura is the villain's daughter in *Flash Gordon.* Three mildly happy babies for the Disney association. Minus some baby points if you gender flip it to Aurelius, King Arthur's uncle.

Austin Powers, international man of mystery, has a name that hails from the Latin Augustine, meaning magic, dignity, or venerable. There's a purple kangaroo character in the animated series *The Backyardigans.* Sean Astin is another reference. Yeah, baby!

Ava see Eve. Ava is #4 in 2015.

Avery Brooks plays Ben Sisko. This ranked at #13 in 2015…but only for a girl. Oddly, Ben ranked the same.

Baelfire, often abbreviated to "Bae," is the son of Rumplestiltskin in *Once Upon a Time.* It's a demon name, and thus a lovely label for a rambunctious toddler.

Balin is a dwarf in *The Hobbit,* named for the knight of King Arthur's court. Both can kick butt at least. Balinor Buckhannah, a Crown Prince of *The Sword of Shannara,* may be a relation.

Balthamos is an angel in the *Golden Compass* series. "Bal" means lord, while "thamos" means hidden or secret. Interesting but a bear to spell.

"1943 – the year after Disney released *Bambi* – was the first year in American history in which at least five baby Bambis were born" (Wolfers).Bambi, Italian for baby girl, is now permanently associated with the Disney deer and widely considered a flimsy, even trashy name. There's also Bambi Berenbaum, a character from *The X-Files.*

Barak, Earl of Trellheim is a hero of *The Belgariad.* There's a Bible hero of this name, which is a variant on Baruch, Blessed. And now there's a president…

Barbara has a bit of an odd origin, as it's from the Greek *barbaros* meaning foreign or strange. The medieval British named many young women after the 3rd century martyr St Barbara, a protectress against fire and lightning. Barbara Gordon was Batgirl and Oracle, while Barbara Wright, a teacher, was one of the original *Doctor Who* companions. Barbara Morgan was an astronaut on STS-118.

Bard means singer, referencing the ancient profession. He's also the archer hero of The Hobbit. Both of these seem more appropriate for a D&D knockoff character than a child.

Barney Drew is a child hero of *The Dark is Rising*. It was always a real name, but after the town drunk on *The Simpsons* and the purple dinosaur, there's some serious baggage. Meaning strong as a bear, it's a diminutive of Barnaby

Barry is Irish for Fair haired or spear. Barry Allen is the obvious namesake as the superhero the Flash. Three happy babies, as it's a bit unusual.

Bartemius means son of Timius. In the New Testament Jesus pronounces him healed by his faith. Bartemius "Barty" Crouch, Sr. and Jr. are villains in Harry Potter. *The Bartemius Trilogy* is another popular children's series. An unusual and clunky choice, likely more Biblical than fantasy.

Bartholomew is more popular since *The Simpsons*. He's also a Dr. Seuss character, while Bartolome is a vampire character in the *Anita Blake* books.

Baruch is an angel in the *Golden Compass* series. It's a Jewish name meaning "Blessed." There was a Baruch in the New Testament, who was a prophet.

Basil is the great mouse detective. Take your pick – mouse detective or herb as your baby's namesake. Certainly a spicy choice. Another famously played Sherlock Holmes in an early television show.

Bast, Egyptian cat goddess, appears in *The Sandman* and in the *Kane Chronicles* Bast has also appeared in issues of *Wonder Woman* and *Hawkgirl.* Further, a male Bast is a clever fae in Patrick Rothfuss's *The Kingkiller Chronicle.* One must note this is a the first syllable of a rude word in English.

The name Bathilda means heroine in Germany, bestowed on Bathilda Bagshot, author of *A History of Magic* in *Harry Potter.* Good meaning, obscure name choice.

Queen Bavmorda, villainess of *Willow*, has a name that casts her as a cousin of Mordred and Voldemort. Good to know they gender-flip.

BB-8 is the sweet baby droid of *Star Wars VII.* Works as a nickname, especially if the kid has a really round bottom.

Bean from the *Ender's Game* series is so-named for his tiny size. He's greatly efficient, a hero and vegetable in one…

Beatrice is Latin for bringer of joy. Dante's guide through Paradise in the *Divine Comedy*, Beatrice is also a major character in Lemony Snicket's *A Series of Unfortunate Events*, though she's dead. Beatrice Prior is the heroine of the dystopian *Divergent* trilogy by Veronica Roth, though she goes by Tris. Bea is also the leader of *Firefly*'s New Resistance, who joins the crew in the comic *Serenity: Leaves on the Wind.* Beatrix Potter would add class to any name. Five happy babies.

Bedivere, a knight of the round table in myth and Monty Python, is probably not the best namesake.

Along with Lucifer and Azazel, Beelzebub was the third King of Hell in Neil Gaiman's *The Sandman* series.

He's the Lord of the Flies in the book of that name. So if this is your kid, just change his diaper already!

Beetee is derived from the energy measurement BtU, for an extra geeky *Hunger Games* name.

Belladonna Took, Bilbo's mother, has a name that means "beautiful lady" or poison, depending. She's also a very powerful sorceress and chosen one in Anne Bishop's books. Very multifaceted.

Bellatrix Lestrange is the evil mad lady of *Harry Potter*. Her name means "female warrior" in Latin and is a star in the constellation Orion. The Harry Potter part is hard to live down though.

Belle: Disney's Beauty and the Beast or Twilight's Bella. It means beautiful and is often short for Isabelle or Annabelle. Not terri-belle.

Bellonda is a priestess of Dune. The "bell" probably means war, not beauty.

Bender, the drunken robot on *Futurama* is appropriately named. You might shorten it to Ben. But you shouldn't.

Benedict is a prince of Amber in *The Chronicles of Amber*. The name means "blessing" and shortens to "Ben."

Benjamin, whose Biblical name means son of the right hand, is actually the middle name of Marvel Hero Spider-man aka Peter Benjamin Parker. There's also Commander Benjamin Sisko

Another variant appears with Bennett Halverson on *Dollhouse* and Claire Bennet (*Heroes*). There's Ben Linus

(*Lost*) and Ben Jackson (*Doctor Who* companion). Benjy and Frankie are the mice that Arthur Dent encounters on Magrathea in *Hitchhiker's Guide*. There's Obi-Wan's alias and a Ben in *The Maze Runner*.

Benjamin Franklin was a scientist and inventor as well as politician. Sir Benjamin Thompson, count von Rumford was an American-born British physicist and inventor who founded the Royal Institution of Great Britain. There's science fiction author Ben Bova too.

Beorn the "skin-changer" of *The Hobbit* was born to be awesome. He's borne a name that reflects that.

Beowulf likely means "bee wolf" (a nickname for "bear"). He was a hero-king who slew monsters and dragons. Sadly, there's little call for that nowadays.

Beren, an ancient hero and Aragorn's ancestor in Middle Earth, has a name that means "brave" in Sindarin. He was also known as BerenErchamion, 'the One-handed', and Beren Camlost, 'the Empty-handed' after he got his hand bitten off being much too brave. Always a risk.

Animal Man is Bernhard "Buddy" Baker. Bernard is a cruel villain in the *Ender's Game* series and clever, sweet Bernadette stars in *Big Bang Theory*. It means "strong as a bear."

Bert is a main character in the *Anita Blake* books. And boyfriend to Mary Poppins. And perhaps boyfriend to Ernie. Often short for Bertram (an evil genius on *Family Guy* and also Bertram Wilberforce Wooster, a character from the *Jeeves* series by P. G. Wodehouse). Bertram is Germanic, from *berht* ("bright") and *hramn* ("raven").

Bertha is a *Pokémon* character, while Big Bertha is in

comic books. Unfortunately, the name is rather linked with the adjective.

Beru from *Star Wars* is Luke's aunt. With a name so unattractive that it's unclear how she got Uncle Owen.

B'Etor from *Star Trek: TNG* is better than some names…but not many.

Betsy, Betty see Elizabeth.

Like author Beverly Cleary, Beverly Crusher's name means "from the beaver meadow." Who knew?

Bianca, meaning white, appears in Shakespeare's *The Taming of the Shrew* and *Othello.* Bianca di Angelo is the name of a heroine in *Percy Jackson.* Bianca Solderini is a vampire in Anne Rice's *The Vampire Chronicles* series. She's also a *Pokémon* character and appears in Disney's *The Rescuers.* The English variant is Blanche, appearing in several fairytale adaptations. There's also Blanchefleur, Percival's wife in Arthurian legend.

Bilbo Baggins has four movies now and a theme song as well. Action figures and keychains. What he doesn't have is a name that doesn't sound like a punchy joke.

Princess Bitterblue of Kristin Cashore's *Graceling* has an ill-fated childhood, starting with her naming.

Blade is the title character from the *Blade* vampire movies, played by Wesley Snipes and another appears in the TV series *Community* and on *Masters of the Universe.*. It's certainly edgy and cool…though it may encourage him to play with scissors.

Blaise Zabini is a Slytherin student in Harry's year.

Bleys is a prince of Amber in *The Chronicles of Amber.* No one will ever spell it right.

Blart Versenwald III was a top genetic engineer, and a man who could never keep his mind on the job at hand in *Hitchhiker's Guide.*

Blight, the Quarter Quell male tribute for District Seven in *The Hunger Games*, has a terrible terrible name. Prophetically, he is killed early when he's blinded by blood rain.

Bo is the talking skull of *The Dresden Files.* This could be short for almost anything…try flipping through the B's.

Bofur and Bombur (don't forget Bifur!) are dwarves in *The Hobbit.* Not the best named ones though.

Bonnie Burton is a *Star Wars* creator and Bonnie J. Dunbar was an astronaut on many flights, though they didn't get many scifi namesakes. The first Arrowette (properly known as Miss Arrowette) is Bonnie King, There are more in *The Hunger Games* and *The Vampire Diaries.*

Bonzo from the *Ender's Game* series is a villain. Sure sounds like a clown though. At least the kid will have some options. Goes great with bedtime stories featuring Ronald Reagan.

Boomer is a pilot on *Battlestar Galactica,* and a Cylon on the new version. A name that comes with sound effects built in.

Boromir dies. He turns traitor and dies. Consider that.

Bowerick Wowbagger was not born immortal but became thus due to an accident with "an irrational particle accelerator, a liquid lunch, and a pair of rubber bands" in *Hitchhiker's Guide*. Then he had to spend eternity named Bowerick.

Boxey is the wonder kid on old and new *Battlestar Galactica*. Sounds like he lives under a bridge though.

Independence Day offers Brent Spiner as rather mad scientist Dr. Brackish Okun. A rather stinking name.

Bradley James plays Arthur Pendragon on *Merlin*. The name means "broad wood" in Old English. Could be worse. There's also Brad Follmer, an FBI character from *The X-Files* or Brad Majors from *Rocky Horror*. Marion Zimmer Bradley is a celebrated author.

Bram Stoker wrote *Dracula*. It's short for the Biblical Abraham. For variants, Brom is Eragon's first mentor in the *Inheritance Cycle*. Brom Bones is the villain of the Headless Horseman short story. And Bronn is Tyrion's immoral sidekick in *Game of Thrones*.

Brand, prince of Amber in *The Chronicles of Amber* (also an ancestor of the heroic Bard of *The Hobbit*) has a name that may lead to branding jokes. May as well call him Wal-Mart.

Brandon, "beacon hill" or "hill covered with the broom plant," is popular enough. The Welsh/Irish version means Raven. There's Bran Stark of *Game of Thrones* – In 2014, four boys were named after him (Poladian). Brandon Sanderson, author of the Mistborn series. Brendan "Hot Dog" Constanza is a pilot on new *Battlestar Galactica*. The variant, Branwen, is a Celtic heroine and also the mom in *A Swiftly Tilting Planet* by

Madeleine L'Engle.

Brent Spiner has a name meaning "dweller near the burnt land." He plays the butt of every joke in *Star Trek*, but this is better than "Data."

Brian means "strong, virtuous, and honorable." Brian Aldissis a popular science fiction author, while O'Brien is the villain of 1984. Brian Krause plays guardian angel Leo Wyatt on *Charmed*.

Brianna is Dustfinger's child in *Inkheart* and the heroine's daughter in *Outlander*. Brienne of Tarth is the warrior woman of *Game of Thrones*. "The noble Brienne rose in popularity, with four babies named after her in 2014" (Poladian). Byron is a vampire character in the *Anita Blake* books.

Briar Moss is a hero in Tamora Pierce's *Circle of Magic* books. He chooses his own name. If you name your kid for nasty thorns, he may do the same. Of course, this is Disney's name for Sleeping Beauty. Still a nasty plant, though.

Bridget appears on *Being Human* US, while another is Saffron's alias on *Firefly*. Brigitta is a tough heroine in the *Kushiel* series by Jacqueline Carey. The name, appropriately, means "resolute strength."

Britt Reid was Green Hornet. The name Britt is a Dutch baby name for a native of Brittany (France) or Britain.

Bruce is Scottish, "from the brushwood thicket." This is a superhero name, used for Bruce Banner and Bruce Wayne. Don't make them angry! Science fiction author Bruce Sterling joins the lineup.

Brutha is a religious leader in Terry Pratchett's Discworld. Sounds brotherly and monkish, but odd.

Buck Rogers in the 25th Century has a macho, heroic name borne by cowboys and space cowboys as well as the dollar bill. It means "male deer," a name used for the animal today. Two happy babies are uncertain whether this is macho or teasable. Likely both.

Buckaroo Banzai, a neurosurgeon/particle physicist, as well as race car driver, rock star and comic book hero, is also an interstellar hero. With a rather silly name.

Buffy Summers kicks butt! However, the joke is that she has a very yuppie, useless name like Bunny or Fluffy, making her ludicrous as a vampire slayer. It's actually short for Elizabeth, believe it or not.

Bungo Baggins, Bilbo's father, sounds like a bumbler.

Buttercup…Along with the Princess Bride character, this is the ironically named cat in *The Hunger Games.* It's a sunny flower, but these characters have their tough side.

Butthead is a nineties *He-Man* villain. Surely someone has used this in all of history…but it shouldn't be you. Of course, baby will laugh gutturally if paired with a friend named Beavis.

Buzz was a clone trooper who served as a member of the 41st Elite Corps during the Clone Wars. Buzz Lightyear shares his name as does "Buzz" Aldrin. But imagine kids make that sound at him all day.

C3PO is a terrible name in over six million forms of communication.

Cadmus was a Greek hero, brother of Europa and founder of a great empire. The name means "He who excels." His namesake is Cadmus Peverell, original owner of the Resurrection Stone in *Harry Potter.* A nice thought but very ancient and very Greek.

Caesar references the great conqueror, guaranteeing your kid a slot as king of the playground. Caesar Flickerman represents the establishment in the world of the *Hunger Games.* Plus, funny hair colors. There's also an *Ender's Game* character. Different spellings get you the Spanish speaking variant Cesar, seen with Cesar Chavez.

Cain was the first murderer in history and thus not a very nice choice though "it's from the Bible." Cain Marco is Juggernaut of the *X-Men* or the last name of one of the Batgirls. Caine is also a prince of Amber in *The Chronicles of Amber.* Kanan Jarrus is the mentor in *Star Wars Rebels.*

Caliban is the villain of *The Tempest,* a Shakespearean fantasy. Of course, he's a nasty, immoral monster.

Calvin means bald, offering the kid some disturbing predestination. Though often the babies start that way…Calvin O'Keefe is the romantic hero of *A Wrinkle in Time* and Calvin Montgomery Rankin is Mimic (X-Men). Crewman Specialist Cally Henderson is a loveable love interest on new *Battlestar Galactica.*

Calypso is a character in *Percy Jackson* and Greek mythology – a lonely demigoddess ensnaring passing travelers. I've heard of desperate for a man, but this is ridiculous. Also portrayed in the *Pirates of the Caribbean* series with teethy excellence by Naoime Harris. Also a popular Caribbean music style.

Camilla was one of the original vampire novels that

started the whole trend, centuries ago. She has a vampire namesake in *The Mortal Instruments.* Camilla Dickinson is an astronomer in Madeline L'Engle's books. There's also the Roman mythological Volscian warrior queen Camilla and the Muppet Camilla the Chicken. Also a character in the video game *Skyrim.* Latin for ceremonial attendant, with quite a variety of series to attend. See Millie.

Candice is a *Pokémon* character while Kandyse McClure plays Officer Anastasia Dualla on new *Battlestar Galactica.* The name means queen, from the New Testament.

Cara "dear or friend" is a character in the *Divergent* trilogy and *The Tomorrow People.* In *The Sword of Truth* by Terry Goodkind, she's a willful fighter. A superhero name, as Kara Thrace is hot pilot Starbuck on new *Battlestar Galactica,* while Kara Kent, Superman's cousin, is Supergirl and Power Girl…DC can't stop at just one. Best if you don't name identical twins Kara and Kara though – one seems sufficient.

Carl (manly, warrior) appears in the Pixar film *Up.* Carl Friedrich Gauss was a German mathematician, one of the greatest in history. Carl Conrad Coreander (Karl Konrad Koreander in German) is the cantankerous bookseller of *The Neverending Story.* Author Karel Čapek invented the term "robot." Karl "Helo" Agathon is a courageous and principled pilot on new *Battlestar Galactica.* Caroline "Carol" Ferris is a character in the DC Comics Universe, a Star Sapphire and love interest of Hal Jordan. Carol Shaw was the first female programmaer and designer.

"Stephen King's *Carrie* came out in 1974, and the film starring Sissy Spacek followed in 1976. Carrie was the ultimate misunderstood outcast, but the name rose in popularity in the 1970s" (MooseRoots). Caroline Forbes of *The Vampire Diaries* and Neil Gaiman's heroic child Coraline are a variant. Wildfire, Carol Vance Martin, is a DC superhero, as is Carol Danvers, Captain Marvel. Karolina is a charming teen heroine of Marvel's *Runaways.* Karl Mueller operates a nightclub, Club Alpha, in New York City in *Mostly Harmless.* Karl Urban played Éomer onscreen. Karla is a queen and heroine in *The Black Jewels Trilogy.* Carl Corey is an alias of Corwin, hero of *The Chronicles of Amber.* Sister Carlotta is Bean's adoptive mother in *Ender's Shadow,* while La Carlotta is a vain prima donna in *Phantom of the Opera.* Carlotta is also the servant in *The Little Mermaid.* See Charles.

Carter Hall is the original Hawkman, an early DC superhero. Carter and Sadie Kane are the stars of Riordan's *The Kane Chronicles.*

Casper the Friendly Ghost has a name that's always been common in Scandinavia, but the 1995 film with hunky star increased the name's popularity in the U.S. (MooseRoots). It means "treasurer."

Caspian: a sea on earth and a Narnian prince, but hard to live down.

Cassandra originally was named for the gloomy prophetess of the Trojan War. This is a minor New *Doctor Who* villainess, but also the name of Wonder Girl and Batgirl (though not the first to bear either title). Cassandra Lang is the daughter of Ant-Man and Stature of the Young Avengers. Cassandra Cillian stars in *The Librarians.* There's also a Cassie in *The Secret Circle.* Princess Cassima is a love interest in *King's Quest,* though something of a damsel in distress. Cassia, a flower, is also the name of the heroine of the YA dystopia *Matched.* There's even Castaspella on *Princess of Power.*

Medtech Cassiopeia (another tragic Greek heroine as well as overbearing mother) appears on original *Battlestar Galactica.*

Castiel ("Shield of God") is an angel name, given to a total jerk of an angel on *Supernatural.* Enough said. Michael and Gabriel seem like more credible names when going the angel route.

Castor and Pollux are the hero twins of Greek myth, brothers to Helen of Troy, though they sound something like a medicine and a chicken. Putting aside the many tragedies of their families, it's awfully kitschy for twins, like Molly and Dolly or something. These characters or their namesakes appear in *Percy Jackson* and *Hunger Games.* And they're stars, too.

Catherine/Catelyn see Katherine

Catra is the villainess of *Princess of Power.* Only if she has a tail.

Cato, villain of *The Hunger Games* and named for Roman history, has had an upswing in popularity lately. It's unclear why…

Dr. Cecilia Reyes is an X-Man, while another Cecelia is an ill-fated tribute and mother of three in *The Hunger Games.* The name means blind – also gloomy. Cecily Herondale is a spunky heroine in *The Infernal Devices* series by Cassandra Clare. Cissie King-Jones becomes the second Arrowette.

Cedric, "bounty" in Celtic, is linked with Cedric Diggory of *Harry Potter.* Of course, he died. Um, spoilers.

Celeborn is Galadriel's husband. I suppose he might

find another flower child…

Ce'Nedra is the princess of *The Belgariad.* A heroine and also spoiled brat. There are so many purely nice princesses…

Cersei Lannister is a terrible woman. We know this. And she walks naked through her home city. And has sex with her brother. And is named for a nasty Greek seducer and villainess. Do you really need more?

Chakotay of *Star Trek: Voyager* has a faked Native American name. The character is from a fictional tribe called the Anurabi and his name means something like "Man Who Walks the Earth But Who Only Sees the Sky" in that language. But all was made up by *Star Trek*. Don't perpetuate this silliness.

Chara, "joy," appears with Chara Alverado, love interest in the webcomic *The Silver Eye* and the manga/anime series *Shugo Chara!* This star appears in a constellation recently named as one of the most likely to host extraterrestrial life.

Charity, a Puritan name with obvious meaning, appears in Charity Burbage, Professor of Muggle Studies at Hogwarts. Of course, she's fed to Lord Voldemort's snake Nagini in *Deathly Hallows,* giving the old-fashioned name a sinister association.

Charles/Carl/Caroline/Charlotte/Carlotta is a name with many variants, all meaning "manly," or perhaps "free man." Charles Xavier leads the *X-Men* of course. Carl William Craft is a creepy murderer on *Dollhouse,* while Charles Gunn is a hero on *Angel.*

Charles Tucker is a likeable hero on *Enterprise.* Charlie (Bella's dad in *Twilight*) and Charlie Pace (*Lost*) also go on the list. A lovely reference appears in the children's book *Charlie and the Chocolate Factory* as well as Charles Wallace Murray, child hero of *A Wrinkle in Time*. Carlos Gutierrez is El Vengador in *Heroes Reborn*. Charlie Weasley is Ron's oldest brother in *Harry Potter*. Charles Beckendorf, a son of Hephaestus who can build almost anything, stars in the later *Percy Jackson* books.

Real life heroes include Charles "Chuck" Yeager, who broke the sound barrier and Charles M. Duke, Jr., capsule communicator during the Apollo 11 Moon landing and Lunar Module Pilot on Apollo 16. He walked on the moon, as did Charles "Pete" Conrad of Apollo 12.There's also science fiction author and host of *Cosmos* Carl Sagan. Charles Dickens wrote possibly the most famous ghost story, *A Christmas Carol*. Charles Babbage is considered the "father of the computer." Charlaine Harris is the author of the *Sookie Stackhouse* books. Carolyn Janice Cherry, better known by the pen name C. J. Cherryh, is a popular science fiction author. Carolines star in *The Vampire Diaries, The Fault in Our Stars, Dollhouse,* and *Portal*. Carlottas sing in *The Phantom of the Opera* and works in Prince Eric's castle in *The Little Mermaid*. There's a Charlotte in *The Princess and the Frog*. Plus the spider. Charlotte was baby name #7 in 2015.

Chase Masterson, actress who plays *DS9*'s Leeta, as well as Buffy/Angel actress Cordelia Chase provide a romantic pair of namesakes, though this really sounds like a stage name. There's also a cheerful teen Chase in Marvel's *Runaways*.

Cheryl means "dear one." Sherrill is a heroine in Mercedes Lackey's *Valdemar* books.

Chester is the first name of Professor Marvel in *The Wizard of Oz*. (It references a British-Roman military camp.) Bet no one will figure that one out.

Chewbacca (of *Star Wars*) may derive from chewing tobacco. Either way, do you want to name your child for a walking carpet? Or a hairball that's looking for a large enough cat? On the other hand, he (she?) will always win at holographic chess.

Chiana is the runaway thief of *Farscape*. Good for children born with no pigment…

China Miéville is a popular author of urban speculative fiction. The name, whether for the country or the dinnerware, seems an odd choice.

Chloe, meaning young shoot, appeared in Greek mythology as an alternative name for the goddess of agriculture and fertility, Demeter, Aside from this original mythology link, Chloe King stars in the US show and book series *The Nine Lives of Chloe King,* while Chloe Sullivan aids Clark Kent on *Smallville*. The name is #16 in 2015.

Christopher (Christ-bearer) and Christine (Christian) have their place in science fiction –There's actors Christopher Eccleston (Ninth Doctor), Christopher Lloyd (*Back to the Future*), and Christopher Lee (Dracula, Saruman). Director Chris Columbus, author Christopher Pike. Fictional characters include Nurse Christine Chapel of *Star Trek,* Christopher "Topher" Brink (the loveable goof on *Dollhouse*) and Jonathan Christopher Morgenstern, a name given to the villain and the hero in *The Mortal Instruments*. Chris Halliwell is the second son of Leo and Piper on *Charmed*. Christopher "Kit" Kellen Rodriguez is the hero of the *Young Wizards* series. Christopher Marlowe wrote *Faust* and many other fantastical plays. He gets entangled with fairyland in *Sandman* comics and in the *Ink and Steel* series by Elizabeth Bear. Christine is the heroine of *The Phantom of the Opera.* And of course one must nod to Christopher Robin from *Winnie the Pooh.*

Chumley is an enormous but quite gentle troll from *Myth Adventures.* Sounds like chum but also like chump.

Cimorene is the smart and independent princess in *The Enchanted Forest Chronicles* by Patricia C. Wrede. Seems plausible, if unlikely.

Cindy appears as Original Cindy of the show *Dark Angel.* Diminutive of Cynthia, Lucinda, and Cinderella. From Mount Cynthus, Cynthia was a name of moon goddess Artemis. Cynthia Von Doom is also the mother of Marvel's Doctor Doom. One critic notes that the Disney film "is largely to blame for the fact that there are around 100 women in their mid-60s – who I like to imagine are trying hard to keep track of their shoes – named Cinderella" (Wolfers).

Cinna, Katniss's friend and stylist in *The Hunger Games,* takes his name from Roman consul Lucius Cornelius Cinna, who led a failed revolution and was murdered in a mutiny of his own soldiers in 84 BC. Plus it's weird.

Clare/Clara means clarity, unsurprisingly, relating to both light and understanding. Clara Oswald is a popular young *Doctor Who* companion, one of many young superheroes with this name. Clary Fray is the heroine of *The Mortal Instruments.* Klara is a superhero called Rose Red in Marvel's *Runaways,* and Claire Bennet is the cheerleader star of *Heroes.* Clara Kendall, Tomorrow Woman, is a DC heroine, Claire Temple is Daredevil's friend, and Clarice Ferguson is the X-Man Blink. There's one on *The Guild.* Marion Zimmer Bradley's Claire Moffat is a powerful and loving heroine. Claire Saunders is a creepy doctor on the show *Dollhouse* and Claire Littleton appears on *Lost.* Claire

Redfield appears in the video game series *Resident Evil* and Claire Danvers in *Morganville Vampires.* Clarisse is a mean girl in Percy Jackson and heroine of *Silence of the Lambs.* Clarence appears in Narnia. Sister Clarice Willow, rather creepy herself, stars on *Caprica.* Idiot twins Cora and Clarice Groan appear in *Gormenghast.* This could gender-flip to Clark, alias of Superman. Major superhero points.

Claudia is a child vampire in Anne Rice's *The Vampire Chronicles* series. Little but creepy. For contrast, Claudie Haigneré was a French astronaut. The name is Biblical for lame. Three happy babies, with the points off for the lame name meaning, so to speak.

Cleo means "pride," "fame" or "glory." Cleo is a young magician from Rio de Janeiro in Rick Riordan's *The Kane Chronicles.* There's also the *Pinocchio* fish. Cleopatra appears in various science fiction adventures – River Song impersonates her on *Doctor Who* for example. Seems like quite a burden for the kid though. Cleophus seems even worse.

A character named Clint appears in *The Maze Runner.* English for "settlement on a hill," or "from the headland estate," the obvious famous bearer is Clint Eastwood. Clint Barton is Hawkeye of *The Avengers.*

Clive Staples Lewis was known as C.S. Lewis, author of *The Chronicles of Narnia.* Be warned of what else C.S. could abbreviate to, though one assumes that must be better than Clive (meaning cliff).

Clyde Langer is a child hero of *The Sarah Jane Adventures* and Clyde is the villain of *Dollhouse.* It's the name of a Scottish river.

Cohen the Barbarian is a hero in Terry Pratchett's

Discworld. The name is an obvious spoof of Conan, a Jewish last name indicating one comes from the priesthood. It still runs the risk of having the kid raiding ancient temples…perhaps doubly so.

Colin (a.k.a. part #223219B) is a small, round, melon-sized, flying security robot in the *Hitchhiker's Guide* novel *Mostly Harmless.* It means child or possibly "victory of the people." Colin Baker played the Sixth Doctor, though he may have been the most disliked. Colin Creevey is a very annoying young wizard in the Harry Potter books. Marion Zimmer Bradley's greatest champion of good, Colin MacLaren, is tied to the *Avalon* series, but appears in modern times. Colm Meaney plays Chief O'Brian on *Deep Space Nine.* Cole Sear sees dead people.

Comet is an astral phenomenon, but between Supergirl's dippy flying horse, Santa's reindeer, and the detergent (plus its rhyme word vomit) this may be the worst name up in the sky.

Conan the Barbarian was an early fantasy hero. It's a real Celtic name, meaning wise, but the barbaric associations are widespread. Plus, when angered or surprised, baby may exclaim "Crom!" constantly. Sir Arthur Conan Doyle is a more elevated namesake. Conina is Cohen the Barbarian's daughter in Terry Pratchett's Discworld. It certainly appears the feminine form of Conan.

Connor is a character in *Percy Jackson* and *Angel.* In the latter, he's the bratty superhero son. In the former, Connor Stoll is a mischievous child of Hermes. Connor is also the name of Superboy. This could also be an homage to John and Sarah Connor of the *Terminator* stories. It's an Irish name of kings, meaning "strong willed," "wise," or possibly "Hound-lover." Also from the Irish Coachuhhar, meaning high desire. Science fiction author Connie Willis can join this list.

1st Lt. Cooper Hawkes (callsign "Jack of Spades") stars in *Space Above and Beyond.* It comes from the last name for barrel maker, of course. Other homages are Sheldon Cooper from *The Big Bang Theory* and Rebekah Cooper of Tamora Pierce's *Provost's Dog* trilogy.

Cora is Regina Mills's mother in *Once Upon a Time* – basically the evil stepgrandmother. It means "maiden" in Greek, often referencing Persephone. Avatar Korra, the protagonist of the series *The Legend of Korra,* is possibly derived from this. Raquel Welch plays Cora Peterson in *Fantastic Voyage.* Idiot twins Cora and Clarice Groan appear in *Gormenghast.* Some of these have gloomy lives.

Coral is a princess in *The Chronicles of Amber.* Coral Thorin appears in Stephen King's *Dark Tower* series. This name, referencing the ocean rock, sounds like you intend her to be a mermaid. Though you might.

Coraline is the awesome kid star heroine invented by Neil Gaiman. However, she, like the original, may get mistaken for "Caroline" a lot.

Cordelia's name means heart. Her most famous namesake, from Shakespeare's fairytalelike *King Lear,* was banished from her father's court because she couldn't lie politely. Cordelia Chase on Buffy shares this characteristic. Cordelia is also a moon of Uranus. Cordelia Delgado appears in Stephen King's *Dark Tower* series. Cordelia Naismith Vorkosigan stars in the *Vorkosigan* novels, while Cordelia Frost is a Marvel comic book character.

Corin is the prince of Archenland in the C.S. Lewis books. Irish for spear-bearer. The bear spearer might be more macho.

Cormac McLaggen is a Hogwarts student who liked Hermione Granger, though he was rather crude. With a meaning of "son of the charioteer," it's an Irish hero name out of mythology, Possibly it's old fashioned enough that it should stay there.

Cornelius is Prince Caspian's dwarf tutor in the C.S. Lewis books. Meanwhile, Cornelius Fudge was the stuffy and inept Minister for Magic in *Harry Potter.* Corny (Cornelius Stone) is the best friend in Holly Black's *Fairie Court.* From the Roman for horn. It really all sounds corny on some level.

Corwin is hero of *The Chronicles of Amber.* His name is Irish for crow.

A filmographer in the *Hunger Games* rebellion, Cressida was originally a woman from the *Iliad* in a love triangle involving members on both sides. It will always be linked with treachery and ill-fated romance.

Crockagor was a reptilian gladiator in the Cauldron on Rattatak during *Star Wars'* Clone Wars. Please don't have a lizard baby.

Crona is from the anime and manga series *Soul Eater.* Likely related to corona, a pretty thought, though an obscure name.

Crystal Norris is a werepanther on *True Blood* who marries Jason Stackhouse in the books. It's a very magical name considering the new age nature of crystals.

Cthulhu is probably derived from the word chthonic meaning subterranean, referencing spirits of the Greek underworld. Lovecraft used this name for his giant ancient evil. One hopes that's the total opposite of your snuggly baby.

Cully is the leader of a second-rate band of outlaws in *The Last Unicorn.* Spelled like bully…

Cuthbert is hero Roland Deschain's childhood best friend in Stephen King's *Dark Tower* series. Also, Cuthbert Binns is the ghostly History of Magic professor. He's known for being terribly dull, which is likely why the author chose it. While the name means "famous" and "bright," it's also terribly old-fashioned. Professor Binns is a boring ghost lecturer stuck in the past and an uninspiring namesake. You could always see right through him...

After Earth stars Will Smith as Cypher Raige, and the hero of the *Sword of Truth* series is Richard Cypher. Of course, the name suggests a hidden secret. It isn't your kid's true parentage, is it?

Cyrus is a *Pokémon* character, while Cyrus Smith (named Cyrus Harding in some English translations) is one of the protagonists of Jules Verne's novel *The Mysterious Island.* It's Persian for sun or throne but has made its way into Americana.

"Dario" means rich or occasionally gift (from dar, to give). Daario is Daenerys's boy-toy on *Game of Thrones,* handsome and charming, but rather superficial.

Daemon Sadi is the demonic hero in *The Black Jewels Trilogy,* while Daemon Knight is a popular author. There's another in *The Vampire Diaries.* The name certainly means demon, or perhaps guardian spirit, so one wonders why this was ever a good name choice. It seems to have caught on, though.

Daenerys was used for 21 baby girls in 2012 while one of the character's titles, Khaleesi, was given to 146 baby girls. It's arguable which is closer to a "real" name. Certainly, both seem like an utter pain for teachers to spell. And consider how many years you'd have to wait before showing your kid the scenes where she's abused by her brother and husband…

Daeron is the name of several *Game of Thrones* Targaryen kings, as well as King Thingol's loremaster and minstrel in Middle Earth. This spelling seems a bit archaic compared with Daren, Gaelic for great. To go stranger, Dairine "Dair" E. Callahan is a heroine of the *Young Wizards* series.

Daisy is an ex-movie star in *Dead Like Me,* a duck in Disney, a distressed damsel in Super Mario, a selfish jerk in *The Great Gatsby*, and a pathetic kitchen maid on *Downtown Abbey.* Daisy was also the eighth child of Samwise Gamgee. Of course, since Daisy Ridley plays young Jedi Rey in *Star Wars VII* and Daisy Johnson stars in *Agents of SHIELD,* it also works for a superheroine. It's a sunny, friendly flower. But do you want to be named for a set of cut-off shorts?

Daja Kisubo is a heroine in Tamora Pierce's *Circle of Magic* books. She may the token black lesbian, but she utterly kicks butt. The name is related to Dayanara, bird of prey. A hawk is certainly a bold namesake.

Dakota ("friendly") is a character in Percy Jackson. Dakota Fanning starred in *The Golden Compass.* It seems a trendy movie star name, clearly named for the state and/or Native American nation originally from Mississippi – some say people were bored with the state so they split it in two…still boring.

Dale Arden is the heroine of *Flash Gordon.* The name appears just about nowhere else, though.

Damian (one who tames; subdues) appropriately stars in horror films *The Exorcist* and *The Omen.* There's a Damien in the fantasy series *House of Night* and another in the *Anita Blake* books. He's one of the Robins for the DC Comics character Batman, as well as Batman's son.

Daniel means "God is my judge," as he's a Bible hero. He's also a knight in Arthurian legend. There's Danny, the Champion of the World from Roald Dahl. Dan Streetmentioner, Author of *Time Traveler's Handbook of 1001 Tense Formations* in *Hitchhiker's Guide.* On *Angel* and *Buffy,* Daniel Holtz is a villain, while Daniel Osborne is the real name of cool guy Oz, a fit boyfriend for heroine Willow Danielle Rosenberg. Daniel LaRusso is the Karate Kid. Daniel Hall is from the *Sandman* comic book series written by Neil Gaiman. Dan the Dyna-Mite is a Golden Age teen-aged superhero published by DC Comics. Danny Rand is Marvel's Iron Fist. Daniel Jackson is one of the heroes of *Stargate* (film and show). Daniel Graystone is Zoe's father on *Caprica.* Danielle Moonstar is Mirage in *X-Men,* while characters called Danny appear in *Being Human* (US), *Lost, and The 39 Clues.* Finally, Daniel Handler is the real name of children's author Lemony Snicket, though he often denies this. If you must go strange, Da'an is an alien name in *Earth: Final Conflict.*

Dana means "from Denmark." Of course there's Dana Scully from *The X-Files.* Dana Barrett is possessed on *Ghostbusters.* Also Dana Freeling, a character in *Poltergeist.* Dana Polk, smart horror heroine in *The Cabin in the Woods.* D'Anna Biers is a Cylon on new *Battlestar Galactica.*

Danika Bellefleur is a part-fairy on *True Blood.* She gets eaten. Nonetheless, it's a pretty name, Slavic for morning star.

Dante, enduring, means naming for poet Dante Alighieri who wrote *The Divine Comedy.* Sounds a bit like you're preparing him for a journey to hell. Well, he's going to enroll in kindergarten…

Ermintrude hates her pompous name. On the island of the Terry Pratchett book *Nation,* she changes it to the more assertive Daphne. This is a popular British name from the laurel of Greek myth.

In Khmer, Thai and Lao, Dara is a male or female name meaning "star." In Hebrew, Dara means compassion or pearl of wisdom. In Punjabi, Dara means "leader," in Persian. Dara is a boy's name meaning "wealthy." Dara is a love interest in *The Chronicles of Amber.*

Daren is an English name, meaning "great." Darenthallis is a hero in Mercedes Lackey's Valdemar books, but Daren is likely the better choice. In *The Fionavar Tapestry,* Darien is a child of hero and villain, poised between dark and light.

The name Darius is Biblical for "He that informs himself." Sounds like a smarty-pants. Of course, Darius the Great was a Persian king. He's also a friendly Peacekeeper in *The Hunger Games.* More characters appear in the series *House of Night* (PC Cast), the *Ascendance* trilogy by Jennifer A. Nielsen, and the video game *League of Legends.*

Darryl Morris is the police contact on *Charmed.* It's French for open. Open Sesame, perhaps? The name

Derrial Book (the shepherd on *Firefly*) is Whedon's adaptation of Darryl. This reference to open spaces of the frontier is more appropriate than dull Henry Evans, his birth name.

Darken Rahl is a villain in *The Sword of Truth* by Terry Goodkind. I blame his parents for naming him Darken. Or possibly the author, who was likely brainstorming villain names.

Darth is admittedly worse than Darken. I mean, when people say "My boss is Darth Vader," they're generally not being literal… "The last time more than four boys were given the name Darth was when seven were born in 1978 – a year after the release of the original *Star Wars* film" (Holeman). Vader (father) was actually a relatively popular female name in the early 1900s, though there haven't been more than four girls called this since 1925 (Holeman).

Data: Your kid is a naïve android learning to be human? Even if this is true, he'd probably prefer a human name. Plus, your child's doctor won't know whether to pronounce it as "Data" or "Data."

"Just what do you think you're doing, Dave?" David is a Biblical name, meaning beloved, and going to its great hero king. David Tennant and David Boreanaz are some of the most popular actors in geek fandom. Interstellar Alliance President John Sheridan and his wife Delenn of *Babylon 5* have a son of this name. Dave Lister is the scruffy hero of *Red Dwarf*. Dave Martyniuk (later called Davor) is an ordinary guy turned hero in *The Fionavar Tapestry*. David Alleyne is Prodigy of the Young Avengers. David is Prince Charming in *Once Upon a Time*. Dr. Dave Bowman stars in *2001: A Space Odyssey*.

Science fiction authors include David Brin, David Gerrold, Dave Duncan, and David Weber. David Scott was an astronaut on Gemini 8, Apollo 9, and Apollo 15. He walked on the moon. Of course, there's also Davy Jones and his locker, in *Pirates of the Caribbean* and the sea folklore that went before it. Variants include Davis (Slipstream from *X-Men*) and Davos Seaworth from *Game of Thrones.* Or if you're feeling more creative than sensible, there's always supervillain cyborg Davros from *Doctor Who.*

Dawn is Buffy's sister and an emerging heroine on the television show. Also a Pokémon character. "Dawn [as in the sunrise] is forever young, never aging, never dying, she follows her destiny and sees generation succeed generation," as Jean Chevalier and Alain Gheerbrant explain in *A Dictionary of Symbols* (275).

Daystar is the heroically-named prince from *The Enchanted Forest Chronicles* by Patricia C. Wrede. The day star is the sun. More romantic prince than sensible child. Dweeb!!!!!!!!!!!!!

Richard Dean Anderson stars in *Stargate,* and Dean Thomas is a likeable Harry Potter character. Dean Winchester stars on *Supernatural.* Science fiction authors Dean R. Koontz, Dean Wesley Smith, and Alan Dean Foster complete the list. From the Greek word "Decanos" which means "Monk or dignitary in charge of ten others," the Latin "Decanum," which means "Chief of a group of ten," Old English for valley and Hebrew for law. Quite a sturdy collection. Plus the kid will likely excel at counting on his fingers.

Deanna Troi is named for a variant on Diane. She's something of a bubble-head, though.

Death, Delirium, Desire, Despair, Destiny, Destruction, and Dream are the main characters of Neil

Gaiman's *The Sandman.* I'm sure their parents had good intentions…

Deckard (Harrison Ford) stars in *Blade Runner.* It's a German surname, meaning "roof-coverer." Not the best occupation, but it may come with a side of action hero. Also, Deckard Cain was a Horadric scholar in the *Diablo* video game universe. Very handy if your world is overrun with demons, but let's hope it doesn't come to that.

Dedalus Diggle – If you need to ask why not, you're beyond help. In Greek myth, he survived but his kid bit it from one of his inventions.

DeForest obviously means "of the forest." It's Trekkie, but terribly old-fashioned.

Dejah Thoris is a princess of Mars invented by Edgar Rice Burroughs I'm having Déjà vu…

Detective Del Spooner may be the dumbest dumb person in the world, though he's played by Will Smith in *I, Robot.*

Delenn is the heroine of *Babylon 5*. Perhaps the Minbari spell her name correctly, but no earth teacher ever will. Dylan could work…

Denethor might take his place beside your kid's list of dinosaurs. But in *Lord of the Rings* I wouldn't call him a good guy…

Denna comes from Rothfuss's *The Kingkiller Chronicle*, in which she's the most desirable and clever woman anywhere. She's a villainess-heroine in Goodkind's books. It's obscure, but it *could* be an earth name related to Dinah or Dena (Hebrew for slender)…at least until you read

Sword of Truth.

Dennis is the lovable ghost haunting Cordelia on *Angel.* Dennis Creevey is a young Muggle-born Gryffindor student, while Dennys Murry is one of the heroine's brothers in *A Wrinkle in Time* and the "normal" kids in their sciency family. There's also the peasant in *Monty Python and the Holy Grail.* And don't forget *Star Trek* actress Denise Crosby, Tasha Yar. The name comes from the Christian saint named Dionysius after the Greek god of wine.

There's a Derek on *Teen Wolf.* It's from Theodoric, Germanic for "people-ruler."

Desmond Hume appears in *Lost.* It's Inuit meaning Boss. Desna in *Avatar* may be a variant.

Devan is the chronicler and straight man in Patrick Rothfuss's *The Kingkiller Chronicle.* It appropriately means servant or poet…best go with the latter.

There's a Dexter in *Star Wars* if you're desperate to get the force in somewhere. It means "dyer" or "right," depending on origin. Of course, the television serial killing hero complicates matters.

Diane, the classic Roman name for the goddess of the hunt, has a few namesakes. Diana is Wonder Woman's real name. The superhero Black Canary is named Dinah. There's Diana Muldaur, the actress who played a doctor of *Star Trek: The Next Generation.* Diana Fowley, an FBI character from *The X-Files.* Diana Wynne Jones, author of *Howl's Moving Castle* and many other fantasy works. Diane Duane, author of the *Young Wizards.* Dionah appears in "And Another Thing..." by Eoin Colfer. Another Dionah is one of Zaphod Beeblebrox's favorite Singer/Prostitutes in *Hitchhiker's Guide. Baccano!* has a Dian.

Dilbert: A real English name, meaning "day-bright," but one permanently associated with the comic. Other available names include Catbert, Dogbert, and Shubert.

Digory Kirke of Narnia is the star of *The Magician's Nephew*, while Cedric Diggory from *Harry Potter* shares this name. Likely related to the Norse Digby: "town by the ditch."

Dilys Derwent is a healer in *Harry Potter.* Means "genuine" in Welsh, but genuinely a strange choice if you're not from there.

Dindrane is the sister of Percival in Arthurian legend. Not to be confused with "don't drain."

Dink from the *Ender's Game* series is, one hopes, a nickname not a birth-certificate name.

Dirk Gently appears in Douglas Adams' *Dirk Gently's Holistic Detective Agency.* Dirk is also a Mercedes Lackey character. Dirk Benedict plays Starbuck on original *Battlestar Galactica.* Dirk Cresswell is the Muggle-born Head of the Goblin Liaison Office in *Harry Potter.* Some might argue that we live in a society without the need for crude weaponry such as the dagger or dirk.

Diva Plavalaguna is a blue alien opera singer in *The Fifth Element.* Beware of names that self-advertise.

Dobby is a free elf! Dobby is also the dork of the series and dead besides.

The Doctor is the name (as far as we know) of beloved characters on *Doctor Who* and one know-it-all on

Voyager. I think your kid would appreciate a real name, though. Save this for his chatroom handle. Plus, if you try "Doctor Who," this will likely become "Doctor Poo" his first year.

Dolia is a hero of *The Chronicles of Prydain.* Dahlia or Dolly seems a bit more standard, unless one is actually a doleful flower.

Dolores Jane Umbridge is a very very nasty lady in *Harry Potter.* The name means pain, and she can dole it out.

Dominic Keating plays Malcolm Reed on *Star Trek: Enterprise* and Dominic Monaghan plays Merry in *Lord of the Rings.* A Catholic British name and obscure, meaning "of our Lord," but acceptable.

Donald "Deke" Slayton was one of the original Mercury Seven Astronauts, who oversaw the Apollo program. Donn F. Eisele was an astronaut on Apollo 7. There's science fiction author Donald A. Wollheim, founder of DAW books. And then there's the duck. It's all Scottish for "great chief."

Wonder Girl was Donna Troy, before she forged a new superhero identity as Troia. Donna Noble is a beloved *Doctor Who* companion. Donna Gilchrist hails from *Being Human* (US). Dr. Donna Eleese is Sam's wife on *Quantum Leap.* Donna Cavanagh (Foxglove) is a lesbian writer and musician in *The Sandman.* Dona Bailey was the first woman to design an arcade game, *Centipede.* The name is Italian for lady. An interesting variety of references.

Doreen is the delightful Marvel heroine Squirrel Girl. Her name, like Dora or Pandora, means "gift."

Dorian is a hero in *The Elder Scrolls*, while Dorian Gregory plays police contact Darryl Morris on *Charmed.* Dorian Grey never ages in his classic novel. Also Dori is a dwarf in *The Hobbit*. Greek for "from Doria."

Dorothy, "gift of God," was very popular in the 1930s, presumably in the wake of the movie. C'mon. We all know which movie. Doctor Who had two companions called Dorothy, though one was nicknamed Dodo and the other Ace. While the first is something of a wimp, the second is a delightful punk teen with explosives. Dorothea SaDiablo is the villainess in *The Black Jewels Trilogy*. Dorothy M. Metcalf-Lindenburger was an astronaut on STS-131, while Dorothy Crowfoot Hodgkin advanced the x-ray crystallography technique all the way back in the 1940s. This is a terribly varied list, but even *Doctor Who* fans will picture the *Wizard of Oz* girl.

Douglas is respectable…if you want to name your kid dark water for some reason (though it is a *Doctor Who* episode title). One is the protagonist of Bradbury's *Dandelion Wine*. Doug Ramsey is Cypher of *X-Men*, while Douglas Adams is always a delightful science fiction homage.

Draco means dragon as the bratty antihero of *Harry Potter* knows. Is he really the best namesake in scifi-fantasy?

Drinian is the captain of the Dawn Treader and advisor to Caspian in the C.S. Lewis books. Sounds drippy.

Drizella is an evil stepsister in Disney's *Cinderella.* Sounds drippier.

Droidbait, designated as CT-00-2010, was a clone

trooper who was killed by enemy drioids in *Star Wars'* Clone Wars, leaving his name prophectic. And just terrible.

The name Drusilla is quite old-fashioned, more Victorian than modern. Literary characters from that era named Drusilla appear in Thomas Hardy's *Jude the Obscure,* Wilkie Collins's *The Moonstone* and Faulkner's *The Unvanquished.* The *Buffy* character is Victorian, but also a murderous, mad vampire.

The Duck Man is a homeless, mad character in Terry Pratchett's Discworld. This name is in fact worse than "The Doctor" though possibly more fun online

Dudley Dursley is the Muggle son of Vernon Dursley and Petunia Evans, first cousin of Harry Potter, while Dudley Doright hails from Bullwinkle. They both seem like silly namesakes, meaning "from the people's meadow."

Dukat is the adversary of *Star Trek: DS9.* Everyone will assume it rhymes with Bucket.

Duma is a fallen angel in *The Sandman.* While this is a real angel name, certainly, the playground kids will notice it's close to Dumb-a.

Dunk (who changes his street name to Ser Duncan the Tall) is a beloved *Game of Thrones* prequel hero. Of course, his nickname sets him up for Dunk the Lunk. There's Duncan Idaho, the only character to appear in all of Frank Herbert's *Dune* novels, and Duncan MacLeod, the immortal protagonist of *Highlander.* And Duncan is the murdered king of *Macbeth.* "There can be only one."

Dureena Nafeel is a talented thief in *Babylon 5: Crusade.*

Possibly a bit too exotic.

Durnik, a blacksmith, is a hero of *The Belgariad.* Still the name sounds like something found in the cracks between walls…or toes.

Dustfinger is a villain of *Inkheart.* Dust-finger. Really.

Dwalin is a dwarf in *The Hobbit.* One assumes he may have been picked on on the playground more than many of his dwarfish companions.

Dworkin Barimen is the mad sorcerer-grandfather in *The Chronicles of Amber.* It sounds like what Dwalin writes on the door when he's working.

Dylan is the name of the captain in the show *Andromeda.* Meaning "son of the wave," it's linked with Welsh poet Dylan Thomas and American folk singer Bob Dylan as well as Celtic myth.

Eccentrica Gallumbits is known as "The Triple-Breasted Whore of Eroticon Six" in *Hitchhiker's Guide.* A disturbing name, image, and profession, all in one.

Echo was a victimized young woman in mythology, as is her *Dollhouse* namesake. Plus the latter is just a codename.Another Echo, designated CT-1409, was a clone trooper who fought during *Star Wars'* Clone Wars and repeated orders in an irritating fashion.

Ector raised King Arthur in legend. The variant Hector, of course, is far more standard.

Edgar "prosperous spear" makes a statement. American Gothic author Edgar Allan Poe was a gloomy guy who died in a gutter, but he was the author of the

American Gothic movement. Edgar Rice Burroughs was author of *Tarzan* and *John Carter of Mars.* Also the nasty bug-guy in *Men in Black.* Prince Edgar is a love interest in *King's Quest,* though originally creepy and green. Edgar Mitchell was an astronaut on Apollo 14 who walked on the moon. Of course, *Men in Black* stars Edgar the Bug

Edmund Pevensie of Narnia starts as a bad kid but learns wisdom and is finally called "the Just." The name means "protector of wealth."

Edna is Giles's wise grandmother in the Buffy comics. Her name is the Anglicized form of the Irish and Scottish name Eithne, "kernel" in Gaelic. It is also related to Eden, the paradise of youth. Edina Monsoon stars in *Absolutely Fabulous.*

Edward "wealthy guardian" is a name of English kings – perhaps that's why in *Enchanted,* Giselle rejects the perfect Prince Edward for ordinary Robert. Early fantasy author Lord Dunsany (1878–1957) was Edward Plunkett. Also known as the "Father of Immunology," Edward Anthony Jenner was an English scientist and is famous for his discovery of smallpox vaccine. Edward White was an astronaut on Gemini 4 who died in the Apollo 1 fire. Also, Edwin "Buzz" Aldrin was an astronaut on Apollo 11. Edwin Hubble built the famous telescope. Edward James Olmos stars in new *Battlestar Galactica* and *Blade Runner.* Eddie is the name of the shipboard computer on the starship Heart of Gold in *Hitchhiker's Guide.* There's also precocious Edward Elric from *Fullmetal Alchemist. Forbidden Planet* offers Dr. Edward Morbius.

"The popularity of Edward did not increase after *Edward Scissorhands* in 1990, but saw slight growth in 2009 possibly due to the popularity of the *Twilight* series" (MooseRoots). You lose points if you name for the romantic stalker-vampire-boyfriend of *Twilight,* Edward

Cullen. Eddard Stark, Ned on *Game of Thrones,* is a made-up variant.

"Effie" is short for the Roman Euphemia, meaning "well spoken," a name popular in the nineteenth century. Saint Euphemia was martyred for her defiance of Rome and her secret allegiance to the Christian faith, while Effie Trinket of *Hunger Games* only survives the series by being believed to be a rebel. She's certainly a little trinket of a person. There's also an Effie on *Skins. The Hunger Games* likely accounts for its recent popularity.

Effrafax of Wug is a sciento-magician in *Hitchhiker's Guide.* And also not a nice name.

Egg (short for Prince Aegon) is a beloved hero of the *Game of Thrones* prequel series. Dr. Egon Spengler is a Ghostbuster. Perhaps they're related? Egg seems more logical for a fetus though.

Egwene al'Vere is a hero in *The Wheel of Time.* Sounds like what you do with leftover eggs.

Eilonwy is the princess of *The Chronicles of Prydain.* Sounds very Welsh. If you're not from there, might go with Ellen.

Elaida is the queen's advisor in *The Wheel of Time.* She probably spent lots of time giving her advice on spelling…

The original Elaine is the Lady of Shalott in Arthurian legend and, for the full spectrum, there's an Elaine in the *Monkey Island* game series. Elayne Trakand is the princess in *The Wheel of Time.* B'Elanna Torres may share this homage. It's a variant on Helen, shining. Eileen Collins was an astronaut on STS-63, STS-84, STS-93, STS-114. Doesn't seem to be popular in fiction, though fine in real life.

Elanor is oldest daughter of Sam Gamgee, while Eleanor Arroway stars in *Contact.* While in *Lord of the Rings,* this is a flower, the English/American name comes from Helen, shining. Elinor is Merida's mom in *Brave* and Meggie's great-aunt in *Inkheart.* Eleni Cooper is a kind mentor in Tamora Pierce's Tortall books. See Ellen, Helen

Elend Venture is the hero ruler of Brandon Sanderson's *Mistborn.* This might mean "The End." It sounds a couple syllables short of a *Lord of the Rings* elf name, and may even be an homage.

Elphaba is the Wicked Witch of the West in *Wicked* – coming from the first syllables of L. Frank Baum, *Wizard of Oz* author. Do you really want a water-soluble, green child?

Elijah Wood, named for the forbidding Old Testament prophet, played Frodo in the beloved films. Elijah "Eli" Bradley is Patriot of the *Young Avengers.* Elijah is #11 in 2015. For a newly popular variant, Ellis is a Middle English version.

Elim is the first name of Cardassian spy Garek in *DS9.* A very slippery character.

Elizabeth, from the Hebrew Elisheba, means either oath of God, or God is satisfied. The most famous was the English queen (or rather queens). Still there are plenty in science fiction with Elizabeth Lochley, commander of Babylon 5, and Dr. Elizabeth Weir in charge of *Stargate: Atlantis.* A similar no-nonsense woman is Elizabeth Shelby from *Star Trek: TNG.* There's Elizabeth "Betsy" Braddock (*X-Men*'s Psyloche), Elizabeth Swann of *Pirates of the Caribbean*, and Elizabeth Shaw of *Prometheus.*

Elizabeth Blackwell born on 3rd February 1821, was the first female doctor in the United States. There's also science fiction author Elizabeth Bear. Elisabeth Sladen (note the variant spelling) was the actress who played beloved feminist *Doctor Who* companion Sarah Jane Smith.

This name obviously has more variants than many. These include Lise (Lise Hampton is a love interest of *Babylon 5* while Lise Meitner was a real-life pioneer in radioactivity), Betty (the first Batgirl, the girlfriend from *Archie* comics, and the ship in *Alien: Resurrection*), Betta (All right, Betta George is a telepathic fish in the *Buffy* comics), Liz (Liz Shaw is a scientist *Doctor Who* companion). Lisbeth Salinger of the Millennium Trilogy. Eliza (Eliza Dushku plays Faith on *Buffy*. And she's the heroine of Andersen's fairytale The Six Swans). Dr. Ellie Arroway (Jodie Foster) stars in *Contact* as Ellie Sattler (Laura Dern) does in *Jurassic Park*. Lisa Morel is Aquagirl. Lisa Braeden hails from *Supernatural*. Elspeth is a heroine in Mercedes Lackey's Valdemar books and there's Princess Elspeth of *Dragonslayer*. Elsa is fast racing skywards in popularity. And to cap it all, another is Buffy.

Ella means "everything" or "fairy maiden." Many heroines of Cinderella adaptations have this name, most famously the one of *Ella Enchanted* by Gail Carson Levine. There's also Ella Dunham, a character on the American TV show, *Fringe*. *Rollerball* stars Maud Adams as Ella. And be warned, there's Ella the harpy in Rick Riordan's *Percy Jackson*. #15 in 2015.

Ellen, a variant on Helen, means "shining one." Ellen Ripley of *Alien* revolutionized the woman warrior action movie. Ellen Tigh is a complicated antihero on new *Battlestar Galactica*. There's also Ellen Harvelle, from CW's *Supernatural*. Astronauts include Ellen Ochoa, Ellen S. Baker, M.D., and Ellison Onizuka.

Elliott ("with strength") is E.T.'s best friend. Keep an eye on his closet, why dontcha?

Elphias Doge is a schoolmate of Albus Dumbledore. Sounds like a cranky old wizard.

Elrond: whether elf or Blues Brother, a questionable choice only valued in the flower child era.

Elroy Jetson, as everyone knows, is the cute kid of the future. Best to stay in the present. It does mean "the king," though.

"There were more than a thousand baby Elsas born last year, making it the 286th most common girl's name. The name had not cracked the top 500 since 1917. The timing of this Elsa boom aligns closely, of course, with the late-2013 release of the hit Disney movie *Frozen*" (Wolfers). It's from Elisheba, meaning either "oath of God" or "God is satisfaction." Also, Ilsa stars in *Casablanca.* Elsa is a nice enough name, but has become increasingly popular due to the character in *Frozen.* Let it go. Or Elsa you may regret it.

Elvis appears in the *Southern Vampire Mysteries* and the novel *Mostly Harmless.* Of course, he's still the same character. Accept no substitutions, not even in your own kid.

Elwyn Brooks "E. B." White wrote *Charlotte's Web* and *Stuart Little*…no wonder he went by E.B. It's Welsh for "fair brow," if you want to know.

Elyan was a knight in Arthurian legend. Sounds weird.

Emily, meaning "work," is #10 in 2015. There's Emily Levison (*Being Human* US), comic book character Emily the Strange, and Emily Saunders, a girl that Ford Prefect had "very fond memories of." in *Hitchhiker's Guide*. Emily Duval stars in *Heroes Reborn* and Amily is a variant in Mercedes Lackey's Valdemar books. See Amelia

Emma, "universal," was #1 in 2015. It has other namesakes than Auntie Em – Emma Peel was *the* sixties action girl. There's the X-Man White Queen (Emma Frost) and Emma of *Once Upon a Time*. Emma Caulfield plays Anya on *Buffy*. Emma Cordelia Carstairs kicks butt in Cassandra Clare's *The Mortal Instruments* and *The Dark Artifices* books. Emma Gilbert is the mermaid protagonist from *H2O: Just Add Water* and Emma Washburne is Zoe's child in the *Serenity* comics. Emmet Cullen and Emmett Lathrop "Doc" Brown from *Back to the Future* could also fit here. The cool car's a bonus.

Emmanuel Goldstein, legendary leader of the party in *1984*. Not a bad name, except for this connection. It means "God is with us" and comes from the Book of Isaiah. His namesake appears in *Hackers*.

Ender from the *Ender's Game* series is really meant to be a nickname. Plus, as *Monty Python* reminds us, your end is your behind.

Engywook (Engywuck in German) and his wife Urgl are a quarrelsome pair of gnomes who live close to the Southern Oracle in *The Neverending Story*. Sounds gnomish indeed.

Eoin Colfer (born 1965) is author of the *Artemis Fowl* series, though an unusual variant as names go.

Éowyn (which means horse-lover, but so does Phillip, so stop sniggering) sounds like a real name, but everyone knows where it's from. Éomer is just as bad. Plus, accent marks… you may get an éarful.

Eragon is the protagonist of the *Inheritance Cycle.* Read the books and absorb how a sixteen-year-old wrote them before you go this route.

Eretria is a capable and wily thief in the *Shannara* books and show. Awkward to spell and to meet in a dark forest.

Eric is the name of X-Men Super-villain/ Magneto AKA Erik Magnus Lehnsherr, as well as the real name of the Phantom of the Opera. He's the Disney prince of *The Little Mermaid.* Stan, Eric, Kyle, and Kenny star in *South Park.* For authors, Eric Arthur Blair was George Orwell's real name. Eric is a vampire in Anne Rice's *The Vampire Chronicles* series and a vampire romantic lead on *True Blood.* The name is Norse for "alone" or "eternal."

Eric Thursley is a young Faustian hero in Terry Pratchett's Discworld, and another Eric is prince of Amber in *The Chronicles of Amber.* Eric Idle was in *Monty Python.* Erica Kravid stars in *Heroes Reborn.* Erica Durance plays Lois on *Smallville,* while Erika is a *Pokémon* character. For a variant, Eriond is a hero-god in the *Belgariad.* Certainly a wide sci-fi range, but quite a few antiheroes.

Ernie Macmillan is a pleasant Hufflepuff student in Harry Potter's year, though everyone will likely think *Sesame Street.* It's short for Ernest, truthful.

There's Eruka from the anime and manga series *Soul Eater.* Sounds like *Charlie and the Chocolate Factory*'s Veruca Salt, possibly the worst name ever.

Erwin Schrödinger, was an Austrian physicist and theoretical biologist. One of the founders of quantum mechanics, he is known for the Schrödinger equation and his brilliant contributions to the wave theory of matter. It means "white sea."

Eska in *Avatar* is named for a creek in Sutton, Alaska. You could likely sneak it over the border…

Eskarina Smith is a feminist hero (and female wizard) in Terry Pratchett's Discworld. Could be Russian, but it's not. Awful lot of syllables…

Esmeralda "emerald" is from Disney's *Hunchback* and the original novel. Did you know she dies after everyone betrays her? The smart, no-nonsense head witch of *Discworld* is Esme Weatherwax. Esmeralda Took was Merry's mother in Tolkien. Another Esme is the villainess of *A Series of Unfortunate Events.*

Estarriol – A mage and best friend of the hero Ged, Called *Vetch,* in *A Wizard of Earthsea.* It's a magical heroic name but certainly sounds made-up.

Estë the Gentle, Lady of Healing and Rest, spouse of Irmo Estel, a childhood name of Aragorn, means hope in elvish. Also means "this" in Spanish. Teasing may follow.

Estella (Bolger) Brandybuck was a Hobbit of the Shire and Fatty's sister. The name means star.

Eternal from the anime and manga series *Soul Eater* has a terribly dramatic name but the teasing will be equally…you get the idea.

Ethan was #4 in2015 and shares a name with the *Mission Impossible* character. Ethan Phillips plays Neelix on *Star Trek Voyager.* Hey, anything's better than Neelix. It means "the gift of the island" … where was he conceived?

Ethel Cripps is the mother of John Dee in *The Sandman*. It's a very old Saxon name from Aethelind, "noble snake" or Aethelthryth "noble and strength." Any serpents in the family?

Eugene Andrew Cernan was an astronaut on Apollo 10 and Apollo 17. He walked on the moon. Eugene Fitzherbert is the prince of *Tangled*. The name means noble or well-born.

Eustace Scrubb is the bratty cousin who only learns after his transformation into a dragon in the *Narnia* books and films. His name is Greek for fruitful. I suppose Narnian grandchildren will follow…

Eve, the first woman, has a name that can also mean evening. Eve appears in the *Sandman* comics and on *Angel* (as mostly a villain). Another is Xena's daughter (also sometimes a villain and sometimes in need of saving). There's an Eve in Neil Gaiman's *The Sandman* series. Eve Myles plays Gwen Cooper, heroine of *Doctor Who* spinoff *Torchwood*. There's also Eve from *WALL-E,* though this is short for Extraterrestrial Vegetation Examiner. Evey Hammond stars in *V for Vendetta*. Eve Baird stars in *The Librarians*. Eva is the mother of Snow White in *Once Upon a Time*. Ava is Gretel. Ava Ayala is Marvel's White Tiger. For an exotic variant, Evadne Cake tells the future in Terry Pratchett's Discworld.

Dr. Everett V. Scott hails from *Rocky Horror,* while Everard is a former Headmaster of Hogwarts. It's an English name, meaning brave.

Eytukan from *Avatar* has a name related to the Na'vi word for leader. Or perhaps it means "a toucan."

Ezekiel Jones stars in *The Librarians*. Others appear in

Divergent and in Jenny Nimmo's *The Children of the Red King.* It means "God Strengthens." Plus, it sounds like "geek."

Ezra means help, a Jewish Bible name. There's one starring as the young gifted hero of *Star Wars Rebels.* As a variant (sort of) there's Erza (Air-ih-zuh) from *Fairy Tail* or Ezri Dax from *Deep Space Nine.*

Faith is a name straight from Puritan values along with Hope, Charity, Prudence, and all the rest. She's the antihero/hero slayer on *Buffy.* "Faith had been on the rise for a decade when Joss used the name, and would peak a few years after the character slayed her first vamp" (appellationmountain).There's also Faith Connors from the game *Mirror's Edge.*

Falkor the luckdragon was the giant puppet in *The Neverending Story* that looked like a shaggy dog dragon. How much hair and drool does the kid have? The original name "Fuchur" in the German novel is derived from Japanese "Fukuryuu" ("lucky dragon"). But it sounded in English…well…sound it out…

Fauna means animals. She's the middle, and least authoritative fairy of Disney's *Sleeping Beauty.* If she works with environmental sciences, she may jump a lot each time her name comes up.

Relating to faith and fairy, girls named Faye appear in *Cowboy Bebop* and *The Secret Circle.*

Felicia means happy. Of course there's Felicia Day from Joss Whedon's works like *Dr. Horrible* and her online show *The Guild.* There's also Felicity from the show *Arrow* and the YA novel *A Great and Terrible Beauty* and another in *Austin Powers 2.* In a gender flip, Felix is a young ice magician in Rick Riordan's *The Kane Chronicles* and Lt. Felix

Gaeta is an officer on new *Battlestar Galactica.* Curly hair not included.

Felurian is the most beautiful woman in the world in Patrick Rothfuss's *The Kingkiller Chronicle.* It's arguable whether she has the most beautiful name or just one that sounds clunky and made-up.

Fenchurch is Arthur Dent's soulmate in *So Long, and Thanks for All the Fish.* She was named after the Fenchurch Street railway station, where she was conceived in the ticket queue. Does your child have a similar origin story or are you just that obsessed with Hitchhiker's Guide?

Fenrir is the ravenous wolf of Norse myth, who lends his name to an evil werewolf in *Harry Potter.* Don't predestine your kid to be an evil werewolf.

Ferdinand (German for peacemaker) is the romantic hero of *The Tempest.* Ferdinand the Faithful and Ferdinand the Unfaithful appear in fairytales. It's certainly a fairytale name…

Fezzik in *The Princess Bride* is a lovable oaf short a few brain cells. You've been warned.

Presenting Fflewddur Fflam, a hero of *The Chronicles of Prydain.* Can you even pronounce Fflewddur Fflam? Neither can I.

Fili is a dwarf in *The Hobbit.* In the film, he's the second hottest, if that's your criteria.

Filifermanhathrhumneits'elhhessaifnth or "Filif" is one of the exchange students in *Wizard's Holiday* in the *Young Wizards* series. It may be the longest and most painful on the list. Of course, if you let the cat loose on the keyboard, you could create your own…

Filius Flitwick is the Charms professor at Hogwarts and possibly a cousin of Fili from *The Hobbit*…

Finnick Odair of *The Hunger Games* takes his name from to finick – "to affect extreme daintiness or refinement," or "to trifle or dawdle." He's hot and gallant, but the name means fussbudget.

Fiona means "white" or "fair." At the moment, the *Shrek* princess is central. There are other namesakes in *The Seven Realms,* Lois Lowry's *The Giver*, and the game *Haunting Ground.* Fiona's a princess in Roger Zelazny's *Amber* series. Riley Finn, Buffy's boyfriend, could be another namesake. This also evokes the Irish epic hero, Finn McCool/Fionn mac Cumhaill. Also, Finn is the stormtrooper everyman in *Star Wars VII.* It beats his original name, FN-2187.

Fiyero Tigelaar is Elphaba's lover in *Wicked.* Sounds fiery, and he's a good guy, but no one will ever spell it.

Fizzgig, a friendly monster from *The Dark Crystal,* sounds like a soft drink. A silly one.

Flash Gordon is a heroic savior of the universe. With shiny teeth and great hair. Still silly. Another Flash is a superhero, and another, a clone trooper in *Star Wars'* Clone Wars.

F'laris, F'noris, and F'lessanis are characters in Anne McCaffrey's *The Dragonriders of Pern.* Sounds F'ishy and F'arfetched.

Flick Ohmsford, the protagonist's brother in *The Sword of Shannara,* was clearly not meant for heroism from the cradle. He even shares a name with the character from *A Bug's Life*.

Flora is a princess in *The Chronicles of Amber* and the bossy fairy from *Sleeping Beauty*. The French variant, Fleur, is a rather wobbly competitor for Harry Potter's Triwizard Cup.

Flynn means "son of the red-haired one," an Irish surname. Flynn Carsen stars in *The Librarians*. There's Flynn Rider, from Disney's *Tangled*. Last names include Kevin and Sam Flynn from Tron and Tron Legacy and of course swashbuckler Errol Flynn.

Fook and Lunkwill are the two programmers chosen to make the great question to Deep Thought on the day of the Great On-Turning in *Hitchhiker's Guide*. You wouldn't really name your kid Fook…

Ford Prefect in *Hitchhiker's Guide* named himself for earth's obvious dominant species, the car. Don't do the same, even though he always knows where his towel is.

Science fiction author Forrest J Ackerman shares a name with Forrest Gump. Hope for the former, lot the latter.

Fortuna is a wicked old witch, who runs a sideshow carnival in *The Last Unicorn*. She's named for the Roman goddess of fortune but is not a nice lady.

Fox McCloud (from the game *Star Fox*) and Fox Mulder from *The X-Files* share this unusual name. Another Fox is a clone commander during the Clone Wars. Your kid may turn out foxy but might also go around quoting Fox News.

Frank/Franklin/Francesca means free man, or sometimes Frenchman. This was the first king of Narnia in the C.S. Lewis books, a hero in *Percy Jackson,* and the middle name of L. Frank Baum, author of *The Wizard of Oz.* Franklin P. Nelson, called Foggy, is Daredevil's best friend. Franklin is the child of Reed Richards and Sue Storm.

There's also science fiction authors Frank Herbert (*Dune*) and Franz Kafka (*The Metamorphosis*). (Warning: naming your child Franz may lead to world wars or stories about depressed proles who turn into bugs.) Frank Borman, Commander of Gemini 7, was an astronaut on Apollo 8 and Franklin Chang-Diaz was an astronaut on more recent missions. Frances Marion was the first successful female screenwriter. Francis Bacon was an early pioneer of the scientific method who created "empiricism" and inspired the scientific revolution.

Frank Bryce, Muggle gardener for the Riddle family (murdered by Lord Voldemort) and Frank Longbottom, father of Neville Longbottom in *Harry Potter.* Frank West appears in the game *Dead Rising,* Francis in the game *Left 4 Dead,* and Franken in the anime and manga series *Soul Eater. Men in Black* stars Frank the Pug. Frankie and Benjy are the mice that Arthur Dent encounters on Magrathea in *Hitchhiker's Guide.* There's Dr. Frank N. Furter from *Rocky Horror,* but I wouldn't let him worry you too much.

"Yabba dabba doo!" Fred is Germanic for peaceful ruler. Of course, for fans of *A Nightmare on Elm Street,* it's anything but. Fred Weasley rocks in *Harry Potter.* Fred W. Haise, Jr. was an astronaut on Apollo 13 and the canceled Apollo 19. Science fiction authors Fred Saberhagen and Frederik Pohl join the list, as does the chatterbox heroine from *Angel,* Winifred "Fred" Burkle. Mrs Winifred Gillyflower is a creepy villaness on *Doctor Who,* however.

Frodo Baggins was popular in the flower child era, at

least…

Fuchsia is the naïve princess in *Gormenghast.* And a very girly color. Of course, her face may turn this shade from playground taunts.

G'Kar (from *Babylon 5*)…G'kidding?

Gabriel ("God is my strength") is an angel and God's messenger. There's Gabriel Summers, Vulcan (the little brother of X-Men Cyclops and Havok). Sylar is brutal Gabriel Gray's fake name on the NBC drama *Heroes.* Gabriel "Gabe" Jones is a Howling Commando. Gabriel is Jonas's foster brother in *The Giver.* Heroines are headed by Xena's best friend Gabrielle, though more appear as the younger sister of Fleur Delacour and mother of the Vampire Lestat. Another is a queen and heroine in *The Black Jewels Trilogy.*

Gaheris, is a son of King Lot and Morgause in Arthurian legend. His brother Gareth has a more popular name, though his other brothers Gawain, Agravaine, and Mordred do not.

Gail Simone redefined feminist comics. In the novel *Mostly Harmless,* Gail Andrews is an astrologer who is interviewed by Trillian and an advisor to the President of the United States. Gail Carson Levine is the author of *Ella Enchanted* and a lengthy series of fairy tale novels. Gender flipping brings the *Hunger Games* love interest Gale, named for the storm that flattens allies and enemies alike.

Gaius "to rejoice" is a character in the show *Merlin,* as well as the first name of *Battlestar Galactica*'s Doctor Baltar. Originally, it was Julius Caesar and Caesar Augustus's name. Others feature in in *The Mists of Avalon* series. Heroic but certainly with its dark side…

Galadriel is queen of the high elves, with a name that made the flower child circuits.

Galahad was the most valiant knight in Arthurian legend. Also famous for chastity and dying tragically young. Surely there are other heroes to pick from…

Galbatorix is the main antagonist in the *Inheritance Cycle*. And, sure, *that's* why you wouldn't pick this one.

Galen was a Greek who became the Roman Empire's greatest physician, authoring more books still in existence than any other ancient Greek (about 20,000 pages available today). He's also the wise wizard of *Babylon 5: Crusade*. Chief Galen Tyrol is the everyman hero of new *Battlestar Galactica*. Galen is a schemer in *Dragonslayer*. Galen Marek/Starkiller appears in the game *Star Wars: The Force Unleashed* series. It means "tranquil." Of course, this is pronounced Gay-len, and the playground kids will notice. Gayle could be a gender-flip.

Galileo Galilei was an amazing scientist. But talk about predetermining your kid's future. What if he wants to go into basketball? (Fortunately, there is a playing position in basketball called The Center. Pray for height and a coach with a Heliocentric worldview.)

Gandalf…we all know it's a name. We all know where it's from (actually the Norse Eddas, then borrowed by Tolkien). Please tell me you won't make your baby be the great white wizard (position already taken by a Southern man fond of linen sheets anyway).

Gareth, son of King Lot and Morgause in Arthurian legend, has become a popular name meaning "strong spear," if a bit medieval. For variants, Belgarath the

Sorcerer is a hero of *The Belgariad.* His descendent, Garion (known later as Belgarion) is the young protagonist of *The Belgariad.* But if you name the kid Belgarath, he'll surely walk around threatening to transform people into frogs….maybe you.

Gargravarr is the custodian of the Total Perspective Vortex on Frogstar World B ("the most totally evil place in the galaxy"), in *Hitchhiker's Guide.* Imagine asking teachers to spell it. Five sad babies.

Garkbit is the Head Waiter at Milliways, the impossible "The Restaurant at the End of the Universe." Points for a name that sounds like vomiting. Five sadder babies.

Garrett Sanford is the Sandman in *The Sandman*, while Garrett Wang played Harry Kim on *ST: Voyager.* There's also villain John Garrett on *Agents of SHIELD.* Garrett is Anglo-Saxon for strong spear…it seems like all the Saxon names mean that. For the shortened version, Gary is a *Pókemon* character. Garrus from the game *Mass Effect* might be a variant, if a weird one. See Gareth.

Gates McFadden played Dr. Crusher on *Star Trek: The Next Generation.* Before this, she worked with the Muppets. This definitely has a stage name quality, more romantic than practical. Two sad babies.

Gawain/Gavin, whose name means "hawk of the battle," is a knight in Arthurian legend. Perhaps if you already have a Lancelot and a Mordred…

Ged is the Archmage of Roke, with possibly the lamest secret magical name ever (his everyday name, Sparrowhawk, is cooler if over-romanticized for our culture). Since one shouldn't say it aloud, one might not want to pass it along.

Gellert Grindelwald – Dark Wizard and owner of the Elder Wand in *Harry Potter.* Hungarian for, yet again, "strong spear." Very German sounding, if you feel the need to name for a *Harry Potter* bad guy with Nazi sympathies. In this case, you may need to seek professional help. Or the kid will.

Gemma Simmons (*Agents of SHIELD*), Gemma Hendrix (*Orphan Black*), and Gemma Doyle (*A Great and Terrible Beauty*) unite in this old-fashioned name, meaning "gem." Somewhere there's a Gemworld looking for them.

Gendry is not the worst character or name choice from *Game of Thrones,* though you could just go with Gene or Geoffrey.

Star Trek creator Gene Roddenberry is a delightful science fiction namesake. Also, Gene Shoemaker was the first astrogeologist. Greek for "well born." There are more than 10,000 other genes on every strand of human DNA, but it would take too long to list them all here.

Men in Black stars Gentle Rosenberg, Arquillian jeweler and Guardian of the Galaxy. A sweet but silly name.

Geordi: We all know Gene Roddenberry took the name George and "science fictioned" it up for Geordi La Forge. Why not revert to George? Or Jeor or Jordan or Geoffrey, possibly. Three sad babies for the obvious connection.

George Takei has been making waves in the SF and F world, long long after playing Sulu. Authors include George R.R. Martin who wrote *Game of Thrones,* early fantasy writer George MacDonald, George Orwell, and

George Lucas. George Washington Carver was a famed American chemist and botanist of course. George Weasley is a major prankster in *Harry Potter.* Other heroes include George Jetson, the character from *Being Human* UK, Faith Lehane's father in *Buffy* comics, and Georgia "George" Lass, protagonist of *Dead Like Me.* Another Georgia/ George is Nancy Drew's pal. George Cooper is a hero and love interest of Tamora Pierce's children's books. Today, George has risen to become the seventh most popular name for a baby boy in Britain following the birth of the Duke and Duchess of Cambridge's son (Poladian). Despite the St. George link, it's Greek for "farmer."

Gérard ("strong spear") is a prince of Amber in *The Chronicles of Amber.* It's normal if you're French but otherwise a bit swashbuckly.

Gertrude ("strong spear" again), or rather, Gert, is a heroine of Marvel's *Runaways.* Gertrude is the countess in *Gormenghast.* Trudy Chacón stars in *Avatar.* Beware ending up like Hamlet's mother.

Gilderoy Lockhart is a jerk in *Harry Potter,* a pompous fool who's shown up in the end. Surely there are better Potter choices.

Gil-Galad was an elven king, of him the poets sadly sing. Your kid might sadly sing too…

Gilgamesh Wulfenbach ("Gil" to his friends) prince of *Girl Genius.* He was raised to be an evil genius and that's likely why he was given such a ponderous name, for the mythic Babylonian hero-king. He does turn out good though…

Gilly was Bilbo's relative and a heroine of *Game of Thrones.* From the Gillyflower, it could be worse. If there's a worse than naming for a semi-spineless girl who has a baby with her father…

Gimli: Really? Really? Why not just name the kid Bilbo and be done with it? Or better yet, have nine boys and name them for all the Tolkien heroes. You can show them off like the Von Trapp children and have them sing songs from the cartoon movie.

Gina Torres played tough, awesome Zoe on *Firefly,* if you'd like a subtle and sneaky homage. Generally short for Virginia, Eugenia, Regina…

Enchanted stars Giselle ("pledge"), who's also heroine of a ballet about a young woman who turns into a maddened, murderous will o' the wisp. Well, it's fantasy, if disturbing. The sad babies are kinda neutral on this one.

Gleep, Skeeve's excitable pet baby dragon only makes this one noise ("Gleep!") in *Myth Adventures.* This might be cute for a baby or fetus, but not so much for the thirty-year-old in heavy counseling.

Glinda was invented by the author of *The Wizard of Oz* as a form of "Glenda." Everyone will know which film you're a fan of, so Glenda (Welsh for pure and good) would be a better way to go.

Gloin is a dwarf in *The Hobbit.* Were you aware that in *Bored of the Rings* he's called Groin? Your kid may be too.

Glory or Gloria has an obvious meaning. It's a lovely thought but there's always a chance kids will dance around chanting the song "Gloria" or someone will tell her Glorificus (Glory) is a major villain on *Buffy.*

The Neverending Story begins with a desperate quest of a

small group – Gluckuk (Ückück in the original German book), a tiny man riding a racing snail; a Nighthob named Whooshwoozool (Wúschwusul) on a bat, and Rockbiter Pyornkrachzark (Pjörnrachzarck). There are times when fictional characters make bad namesakes…this is one.

Gmork is the scary wolf villain and a servant of the power behind the Nothing in *The Neverending Story*. It does have that dark "mor" root (death). Nasty critter.

Godric sounds straight out of the Middle Ages, though it's certainly noble. It's Anglo-Saxon for "rules with God" And implies you expect someone to knight him soon if not king him. Godric Gryffindor is one of the four founders of Hogwarts

Gollum! Gollum! Some babies, indeed, do like a wizened little E.T. Best if you count on the kid growing out of this phase and pick some other name. Something normal and respectable. Like Smeagol. No matter how precious the kid is.

Gordon is better than Flash, admittedly, if you're a nutty space opera fan. There's also Gordon Shumway aka ALF and Gordon Freeman (from the game *Half-Life*). *The Wild Wild West* (original and Will Smith film) stars secret agent Artemus Gordon. Scottish for "spacious fort."

Gortwog gro-Nagorm is an orc in *The Elder Scrolls*. Admit it, before you picked up this book, you hadn't thought of Gortwog as a viable choice. And now, you just can't stop considering….

Gowron rules the Klingons on *Star Trek* and has a very creepy stare. Picture the kid striding into kindergarten and offering to battle for dominance of the class. Now name the kid something less provocative, like Worf.

Grace Holloway was a *Doctor Who* companion, and Grace Lee Whitney played Yeoman Rand. Grace Hopper, inventor of programming language COBOL, is also a United States Navy Rear Admiral. Dr. Grace Augustine stars in *Avatar,* and Grace Park plays Athena, Boomer, and many copies of Number 8 on new *Battlestar Galactica.* A lovely name with a lovely meaning.

Graham is the hero of the *King's Quest* computer games. Graham Humbert is the Huntsman in *Once Upon a Time.* Graham Chapman was in *Monty Python.* Sadly, kids will ignore all of these and tease him about the cracker. This Scottish surname is from the Lincolnshire place name Grantham. So if you're a *Downton Abbey* fan, you can sneak in that reference too.

Graklak gro-Buglump is an orc in *The Elder Scrolls.* I like Gortwog better. It just flies off the tongue…

Grant Ward surprisingly reveals himself as a traitor in *Agents of SHIELD*, while comic book writer Grant Morrison is one of the top in the industry. The name is Scottish for "great. "

Greedo from *Star Wars* was probably named for the word Greedy. Playground kids probably know this.

Ensign Greenbean was on original *Battlestar Galactica.* This sounds like a better name for a fetus. Or a side dish.

Prince Greening Grandemalion (nicknamed Po) of Kristin Cashore's *Graceling* has a clunky pompous name that somehow makes him sound like a gardener. Or someone with a skin discoloration. One sad baby.

Gregory Gregorovitch and Gregory Goyle are both

villains in *Harry Potter.* Gregory is a large green gargoyle in Neil Gaiman's *The Sandman* series. Much better namesakes are Gregory Lestrade of *Sherlock Holmes* and Gregor Mendel, father of genetics. This last may be the namesake of Gregor Samsa – the man who turns into a cockroach. It's from Greek/Latin for watchful…watch out for any insect tendencies in the kid though.

Grendel was a delightfully grotesque monster-villain from *Beowulf.* Like Bilbo or Glinda, this is a fiction name with one big fat association. Unlike them, he's an ugly scary monster who got beat down by Beowulf.

Gretel is German for pearl but everyone's heads will go to Grimms. At least Gretel beat the witch in delightful fifteenth-century girl power.

Grievous served as the Supreme Commander through the *Star Wars* Clone Wars. A grievous choice indeed.

Grizzlor is a villain of *Masters of the Universe.* It's…very memorable, wouldn't you agree?

Gromit is the clever dog of beloved cult series *Wallace & Gromit.* At least Kermit was a real name at one point…

The name Grover is English for "grove dweller," a lovely druid name and a real American name going to people like President Grover Cleveland. Still, everyone's heads will go straight to *Sesame Street,* unless they're big *Percy Jackson* fans and loved the humorous satyr.

Grunthos the Flatulent was the poetmaster of the Azgoths of Kria, writers of the second worst poetry in the universe, just between Paula Nancy Millstone Jennings and the Vogons in *Hitchhiker's Guide.* Picture the birth announcement!

Guinan of *Star Trek* was named for bartender Texas Guinan. So a Wild West bartender and a space bartender with a hat brim larger than the Enterprise?

Guinevere is the ultimate fantasy name, with variants like Gwendolyn, Jennifer, Gwyneth, etc. Gwen Cooper kicks butt on *Torchwood.* Gwen is a character in *Percy Jackson*, while Gwena is a magical horse in Mercedes Lackey's Valdemar books. Ginny Weasley from *Harry Potter* is named the related Ginevra.

Gully Foyle in *The Stars my Destination* is named for Gulliver – both travelers of fantastical worlds. Both a bit outlandish for naming. Plus, no guarantee you'll get the kid back.

Gushie is Project Quantum Leap's head computer programmer. With a silly name.

Guts, hero of the Anime *Berserk,* has a brutal, grotesque name in a world of violence where he lurches about as a reanimated corpse. But we know he's tough.

Guy is a Teutonic name, meaning warrior. Guy Gardner was Green Lantern – or one of them. Guy Montag stars in *Fahrenheit 451*. Tough though a bit generic. Guybrush Threepwood of the game *Monkey Island* is another namesake. Threepwood sounds kind of fun though, doesn't it?

Haggard is a miserable and cruel king, antagonist of in *The Last Unicorn.* And he looks quite haggard too. Surely "Beauty" would be a better choice.

Haley gets her own comet – that's very scifi. Also the rebellious teen on *American Dad.*

Han from *Star Wars* is the ultimate rough and tough bad boy. The variant Hans ("gift from God") is a classic fairytale name from the German Grimm's brother world. It's seen in fairytales like Hans in Luck; Hans My Hedgehog and in fairytale author Hans Christian Andersen as well as the villain prince of *Frozen.* Thanks to *Frozen,* "The evil Prince Hans has also found that his name is rising in popularity. Last year 132 baby boys were named Hans, up from 98 in 2013. (Parents, what were you thinking?)" (Wolfers). Hansel & Gretel is a variant. A logical gender flip is Hannah, a Biblical name that goes to Hufflepuff student Hannah Abbott. Sadly, Hannah is the only one that won't provoke pointing and laughing, singing on the street, or possibly shooting first.

Hank see Henry

The name Harmony means peaceful unity, named as it is after the goddess Harmonia. However, Harmony Kendall on *Buffy* is a vapid and vampy vampire, appropriately nicknamed "harm."

David Beckham's choice of name for his daughter is still influencing parents, with Harper climbing 71 places recently (Poladian) and was #11 in 2015. It's a Middle English name deriving from "harp player," which could nod to Owen Harper on *Torchwood* or Seamus Harper on Gene Roddenberry's *Andromeda.*

Harry/Harriet appears as Miss Hattie in *Despicable Me* and Harriet Jones, *Doctor Who*'s Prime Minister (you know who she is). Harry King is a rough and ready businessman in Terry Pratchett's Discworld, while Harry Holt is an explorer in *Tarzan.* Harry Osborn is the second Green Goblin in *Spider-Man.* Harrison Schmitt was an astronaut on Apollo 17 who walked on the moon. And there's always Harrison Ford.

While the name Haymitch was invented by the author of *The Hunger Games*, the "hay" at the beginning evokes someone who's rather a hayseed. Plus he's a terribly drunken grouch. Hamish, a soundalike, is a variant of Seamus and James. The name means "He who supplants": he who takes the place of another.

Hazel, from the nut tree (a fairy tree) rather than the color, offers its name to heroines in *Percy Jackson* and *The Sandman.* After *The Fault in our Stars,* it gained much popularity. Hazelle is Gale's mom in *The Hunger Games.*

Heather Glenn is Daredevil's girlfriend, and Heather Cameron is Lifeguard of *X-Men.* (Superheroine Lifeguard? Really?) The name references the lovely flower. Pretty and popular, though not a lot of science fiction here. Four happy babies.

The name Hector is probably derived from the Greek *ekhein,* "restrain," and references the self-disciplined prince of Troy. Hector Barbossa is Captain Jack's adversary in *Pirates of the Caribbean,* while Hector Hall is Gaiman's Sandman in *The Sandman.* Hector Ayala is Marvel superhero White Tiger. An old Trojan name you could actually get away with if that's a goal.

Hedwig will bring associations of the transvestite musical *Hedwig and the Angry Inch* as well as Harry Potter's owl. It's German for "fighting in battle" which oddly doesn't connect well with either.

Hekatah is a villainess in *The Black Jewels Trilogy.* Before this, Hekate was the Greek goddess of the crossroads, an empowering neopagan goddess but also a creepy figure. She's a Greek goddess of crones. And dogs. And the underworld. With all her negative connotations, there are far better namesakes. In the sixties, Lilith caught on…

Helen "bright, shining one" was the most beautiful woman in the world and also the wife who ran off from her husband and thus started the Trojan War. One seems to cancel out the other. This name also goes to the First Queen of Narnia. Helena Ravenclaw was treacherous daughter of Rowena Ravenclaw in *Harry Potter*. Eilan/ Helena stars in Bradley's *Priestess of Avalon*. Helena is the young heroine of *Mirrormask*. Admiral Helena Cain is an adversary on new *Battlestar Galactica*. Helena G. Wells is the gender-flipped H.G. Wells in *Warehouse 13*. DC's Huntress is Helena Bertinelli. For variants, Lena Haloway is the heroine of the YA dystopia *Delirium* and butt-kicking dryad Lena Greenwood stars in *Libriomancer*. Lena Headey is Cersei in *Game of Thrones*. Yelena Kondakova was a Russian astronaut on Soyuz TM-20/STS-84. Elena Gilbert is the heroine of *The Vampire Diaries*. Five happy babies until the kid reads *The Iliad*.

Helga is Norse for "holy." Helga Hufflepuff helped found Hogwarts, but this name seems awfully geeky unless you're an actual Viking or ancestor of one.

He-Man is the hero of *Masters of the Universe*. Very macho, but a bit ridiculous.

Henry "estate ruler" is the name of Marvel heroes Beast AKA Henry "Hank" McCoy & Yellowjacket AKA Henry "Hank" Pym. Hal Jordan is Green Lantern. This name went to several English kings – eight in fact – as well as many fictional characters. Shepherd Book from *Firefly* was born Henry Evans, and Buffy's father's name is Hank. Indiana Jones was named Henry Jr.

There's a Henry in *The Princess and the Frog* and one in *Being Human* US. Henry Mills is the young hero in *Once*

Upon a Time and there's *Wizard of Oz*'s Uncle Henry There's kindly Harry Kim from *Star Trek: Voyager,* clever Harry Sullivan (a *Doctor Who* companion), Harry Dresden, and of course, Harry Potter. Between the various nicknames, you have a host of superheroes, though Indiana Jones is enough to do it.

Hera is the queen of the Greek gods, though in most versions she's rather a vengeful shrew and evil stepmother. Her namesake Hera Agathon is the first successful Human/Cylon hybrid on *Battlestar Galactica.* Hera Syndulla, a Twi'lek rebel, stars in *Star Wars Rebels.*

Herbert means "famous army." Herb Jefferson, Jr. played Boomer on *Battlestar Galactica,* while Herbert George Wells was one of the original sf authors.

Hercules is the original brawling strongman, light on brains and sanity as he went mad and slaughtered his own family. Then (possibly more tragically) he was turned into a series of awkward films including a Disney. Hercules variants include Alcide from *True Blood and* detective Hercule Poirot.

Herman Munster brought this name to scifi-fantasy, though today there's also Herman Holden, Vork on *The Guild.* And the author of *Moby Dick* if you're a literary geek. It means "soldier" in German.

Hermes is the Greek god of speed and a character on Futurama. One hopes your kid will be as skilled as the god at running away…

Hermione ("well-born") was the daughter of Helen of Troy in Greek myth. Hermione Granger was named for her (or possibly for Hermes) in the *Harry Potter* novels. While this used to be a stodgy British elderly name, seen in the queen of Shakespeare's *A Winter's Tale* and a heroine of *The Fortunes of Nigel* by Sir Walter Scott, it also appeared as Hermione "Her" Gart, central character in H.D.'s *HERmione* and Hermione Lodge, mother of Veronica in *Archie* comics.

Herrena, the Henna-haired Harridan is a barbarian in Terry Pratchett's Discworld. Sounds like a harridan indeed.

Hippolyta is an amazon queen in myth and *A Midsummer Night's Dream.* Hippolyta "Lyta" Hall is a DC heroine, while another Hippolyta is Wonder Woman's mother. Well, it's heroic, anyway. But the kids will likely notice the "hippo" part.

Hlaalu is a king in *The Elder Scrolls.* His name likely means "hard to pronounce."

Hoban "Wash" Washburne is the lively pilot on *Firefly*. "Hoban" is an Irish surname, meaning "son of Ubain," with the "ban" in "Ubain" meaning white in Gaelic (works for blonds). Since he goes by Wash, he appears to dislike the name.

Hodor. Hodor Hodor Hodor. Don't name for the village idiot. His real name is Walder, from Walter. But, um, don't name for the village idiot.

Holden Caulfield from *Catcher in the Rye* shares a name with a Blade Runner. It means "From the hollow in the valley."

Holly references the plant, perhaps a little more painful on the playground than most flowers, thanks to all the Christmas songs. There's Holly Black, author of *The Spiderwick Chronicles* and other series, or Holly Marshall, author of *Land of the Lost.* Holly Cleary is a waitress at Merlotte's on *True Blood,* while Holly Marie Combs played one of the main character sisters on *Charmed.* Holly/Hilly is the gender-swapping computer (with an IQ of 6000 or possibly 6) on *Red Dwarf.* This last is a fun reference, but the IQ has a big disparity there…

Hope Summers is an *X-Man.* Another Hope is the daughter of the Wasp and Ant-Man. It's a sweet name. Quite optimistic, though superheroines get kidnapped a lot.

Horace ("timekeeper") appears in fantasy as Harry Potter's cowardly teacher Horace Slughorn. Plus, your kid will know if you're a minute late for anything. For a stronger, perhaps sillier sound, Hordak is a villain of *Masters of the Universe.*

Howard and Maria Stark are Iron Man's parents, plus he appears on the show *Agent Carter* as a playboy genius inventor. There's also Howard from *The Big Bang Theory.* In Scandinavian, it means "Noble watchman."

Hubert ("bright mind") is an appropriate moniker for the senile genius of *Futurama.* Cubert is his cloned son. A third generation could be Trubert, if you're so inclined.

Hugh or Hugo means "mind." There's Hugh of Borg and Hugo, the movie character and the author of *The Hunchback of Notre Dame.* Also, Hugo "Hurley" Reyes on *Lost* and Hugo Weaving, who played Elrond and Mr. Smith. Resistance is futile.

Humperdink! Humperdink! Humperdink! Don't.

Hyacinthe is a hero in the *Kushiel* series by Jacqueline Carey. He's sweet as the flower he's named for. In Greek mythology Hyacinthus was a Spartan youth accidentally killed by Apollo, whose blood turned into this flower. Various saints with this name probably came to equally violent ends. There's also Hyacinth Bucket, the social climber on *Keeping Up Appearances.*

Actors Ian Holm (Bilbo) and Ian McKellen (Magneto, Gandalf) add distinction to this name, a variant on John, "God is gracious." There's beloved author Iain M. Banks and Ian Chesterton (*Doctor Who* companion). Ian Grant (Sam Neill) and Ian Malcolm (Jeff Goldblum) star in *Jurassic Park.* Ianto Jones (on *Torchwood*) provides a Welsh variant.

Ignotus Peverell is the original owner of the Invisibility Cloak in Harry Potter's "The Tale of the Three Brothers." While he "wins" the story, his name seems ignominious.

By now everyone knows that Igor is Dr. Frankenstein's henchman. Jokes on this include the movie *Igor, Young Frankenstein* (all right, that's I-gor) and the Discworld books where Igor/Igorina is a profession. Thus probably not a great choice unless you want your kid cranking the winch while the lightning rages overhead. (On the plus side, job security.) Igor Karkaroff, Headmaster of Durmstrang in *Harry Potter and the Goblet of Fire* doesn't improve matters.

Igraine, King Arthur's mother has a classy old-fashioned name, unless kids notice it's close to migrane.

Illyria was an ancient region of the Balkans, which gives its name to a tough ex-god on *Angel.* Shakespeare created the mystical Kingdom of Illyria for *Twelfth Night.* The land of Illyria is also the setting of Lloyd Alexander's *The Illyrian Adventure,* the tale of Vesper Holly, a wealthy orphan and genius who goes on delightful adventures.

Imriel de la Courcel is a hero in the *Kushiel* series by Jacqueline Carey. It's an angel name, "the eloquence of God," and rather obscure – both the bestselling books and the angel. Iriel, light of God, is a priestess of Dune with a similar naming pattern. One sad baby.

Inara Serra is the alluring heroine of *Firefly*. Inara was an obscure Hittite goddess (a Demeter rather than precisely an Aphrodite figure). In "The Anatolian Myth of Illuyanka," nearly the only account left of her, she provided lavish food and drink for the gods, lulling the enemy serpents into a stupor. She charmed the hero and won the day. While it's been used occasionally since the 1990s, Inara's use is a name grew significantly as a result of the television show (appellationmountain).

Indiana …you know the film hero was really named Henry Jones, Jr., and only was nicknamed Indiana after the family dog, right? Go for the former and not the latter. Four sad babies.

Iodine Maccalariat is a heroine in Terry Pratchett's Discworld. She stands out for having parents who value *sounding* like a girl's name over actually being one. Hey, iodine stings. A lot. Just four sad babies – some people likely won't know what iodine is, but too many will.

Iofur Raknison and Iorek Byrnison are bears in the *Golden Compass* series. Their names of course sound far more like friends of Beowulf's who quaff mead than anyone who eats peanut butter sandwiches. Four sad babies, since they plausibly could be your Norse ancestors.

Irene Adler is the automatic association for Irene (all right, not fantasy, but Sherlock Holmes has a very long shadow. For a more direct science connection, Irène Joliot-Curie was the daughter of Marie and Pierre Curie, who served in the French Cabinet as Undersecretary of State for Scientific Research. Irene is Greek for peace, though neither woman seems to have had a sedate life.

Kid Flash's secret identity is Iris West. Iris is also a *Pokémon* character and one of Joss Whedon's women on *Dollhouse* (an evil one!). In *Minority Report*, Dr. Iris Hineman is the creator of PreCrime technology. The name obviously references the flower. Two sad babies for all the eyeball jokes.

Irma Pince is the Hogwarts librarian. Irma Prunesquallor appears in *Gormenghast*. It's a variant on Emma, universal. Of course, Ima and Irma can make many puns with the last name, so watch out. What is a Prunesquallor, anyway?

Isaac Newton and Isaac Asimov make excellent namesakes, depending on your choice of heroes. Isaac Peral was the designer of the first fully operative military submarine. There's also folklore collector Isaac Bashevis Singer, (1902–1991), Isaac from *Teen Wolf*, and Isaac Clarke from the game *Dead Space*. Isaac Vanio is the awesome magician-hero of *Libriomancer*. Isaac nonetheless is something of an old-fashioned Biblical name meaning laughter. There's a chance kids on the playground will add to the mirth.

Isabelle ("pledged to God") is an angelic warrior in the *Mortal Instruments* series. Ysabell from Discworld and Sebell from Anne McCaffrey's *The Dragonriders of Pern* are stranger variants. Isabeau is the heroine of *Ladyhawke*. Sibeal mab Necthana is an Irish prophetess in the Kushiel series by Jacqueline Carey. And Bella Swann likely fits under this header. Isabella is #5 in 2015.

Isolde, Tristan's lover in Arthurian legend, is epic and doomed – like calling the kid Juliet but a bit more obscure. Two sad babies.

Isis was a goddess, who also had a short-lived superhero television show. Seems awkward being an ancient Egyptian goddess in modern America. Sadie is taken over by Isis in Riordan's books – you could try that instead.

Ix is the childhood nickname of Ford Prefect. In English, Ix translates to "boy who is not able satisfactorily to explain what a hrung is, nor why it should choose to collapse on Betelgeuse Seven." It sounds like a letter or mathematical symbol, and it sounds like you've reached nutty levels of fandom if you plan to perpetuate this one. Four sad babies.

Jabba the Hutt …surely you wouldn't name your kid for well-known *Star Wars* villain – and a fat, ugly, gross one! Now we've hit five sad babies.

Jace Wayland is a hero in *The Mortal Instruments.* Of course, it's short for J.C. in his case (Jonathan Christopher), and Jason is another logical variant.

Jack O'Neill and Captain Jack Harkness are the heroes of *Stargate* and *Torchwood* respectively. There's Jack Shephard (*Lost*), Black Jack of *Astro Boy*, and Jackson Hyde, Aqualad. Jack Jackrum is a hero in Terry Pratchett's *Discworld.* Fairytales are stuffed with these, including Jack & the Beanstalk; Jack the Giant Killer; Appalachian Jack Tales; *Legend;* plus more. There are too many authors to list, including Jack London, Jack Vance, and Jackie Tyler. Creepy villains Jack the Ripper and Jack Torrance (*The Shining*) are joined by Jack Skellington (*A Nightmare Before*

Christmas). With all these, even devoted fans may not go instantly to Captain Jack Sparrow. There's also Jacqueline from the anime and manga series *Soul Eater* and several Jackies who are giant-killers too. While Jackson is another option (and #7 in 2015), classically Jack has been short for John (odd as that sounds). Jack is #15 in 2015. Five happy babies with bonus points for so many cool references. Or geeky, as it goes.

Jacob Black is the hot werewolf of *Twilight,* while Jake Sisko grows up as the Commander's son on *Star Trek: DS9*. There's another Jake on *Touch*. Jake Sully stars in *Avatar* and Jake Stone in *The Librarians*. It means "wrestles with God." #11 in 2015.

Jadis is the White Witch in the C.S. Lewis books. Not in any way a nice lady, in fact, not even human.

Jadzia Dax has an alien name, complete with exotic z, though it's better than Jadis.

Jagang is a supervillain tyrant in *The Sword of Truth* by Terry Goodkind. Jangling, jarring, and just a bad idea.

Jaime Lannister is the conflicted antihero of *Game of Thrones*. He's gorgeous and amazing fighter, but then he sleeps with his sister and gets his hand cut off… Jamie Campbell Bower plays Jace, star of *The Mortal Instruments* film. The hero of *Outlander* was named for Jamie McCrimmon, beloved *Doctor Who* companion from the sixties. Jamie De Curry is hero Roland Deschain's companion in Stephen King's *Dark Tower* series. In 2006, DC introduced a new Blue Beetle, teenager Jaime Reyes. Jamie Madrox is Multiple Man of the X-Men. Jamie Bamber plays Apollo on new *Battlestar Galactica*. The name works for either gender – Jaime Sommers is the Bionic Woman. A fun variant on James, below.

James means "He who supplants," a Biblical name for one of the disciples. This name can't be supplanted in SF – it's everywhere! #12 in 2015. James T. Kirk must dominate the James list – he arguably started science fiction television and certainly Star Trek. James Doohan, Scotty, joined him in this and James Marsters, who played Spike, made his own contributions. James Callis plays Gaius Baltar on new *Battlestar Galactica. The Wild Wild West* (original and Will Smith film) stars secret agent James T. West. In comics, *X-Men* hero, Wolverine's real name is James "Logan" Howlett. James "Jim" Barr and Susan Kent-Barr were Golden Age Bulletman and Bulletgirl. There's James "Sawyer" Ford of *Lost.* James Potter was Harry Potter's father and James Norrington, a decent man who doesn't get the girl in *Pirates of the Caribbean.* Jim Nightshade and William Halloway star in Bradbury's "Something Wicked This Way Comes."

Too many authors to list including Robert Jordan (pseudonym of James Oliver Rigney, Jr.), Jim Butcher who wrote *The Dresden Files*, James Blish, and Sir James Matthew Barrie author of *Peter Pan* who seems to have cast himself as villainous Captain James Hook). James "Jim" Lovell was an astronaut on Gemini 7, Gemini 12, Apollo 8, and Apollo 13 (played by Tom Hanks in the latter film). Other astronauts include James A. McDivitt (Commander of Gemini 4 and Apollo 9) and James B. Irwin (Apollo 15). James Prescott Joule was an English physicist who studied the nature of heat particularly the Joule's laws. James Dewey Watson discovered the molecular structure of DNA, and James Watt was the father of the industrial revolution.

Finally, James/Jem is a hero of Cassandra Clare's *The Infernal Devices* and Jim Raynor stars in the *StarCraft* games. Beware of Jiminy Cricket.

Jane Austen didn't write fantasy but she certainly

caters to the geek community. Jane Yolen is an amazing novelist with hundreds of fairytale adaptations, with Jane Lindeskold writing some too. Other Janes are Jane Jetson and Dame Jane Goodall. Jane is Tarzan's girlfriend, Jane Foster is Thor's, and Mary Jane is Spider-Man's. Jane Drew is child heroine of *The Dark is Rising,* and there are more in *Mary Poppins* and *Peter Pan.* Well, you can't beat it for variety. It and the following Janet mean "gift from God" and are varients of John.

Janet L. Kavandi was an astronaut on STS-91, STS-99, STS-104. Another Janet is the heroic doctor on *Stargate.* Also Janet Weiss from *Rocky Horror.* Janet Van Dyne is Wasp of the *Avengers.* Varients include Janice, for Janice Rand of original *Star Trek* and Janice Voss, astronaut on five missions. Janine Melnitz helps the Ghostbusters. Jaenelle Angelline is the chosen one in *The Black Jewels Trilogy.* Five happy babies, but don't take the kid to see *Rocky Horror* for a while…

Jared ("ruling," possibly "rose") entered cult fandom with the flamboyant goblin king of *Labyrinth,* though Jared Padalecki is the actor who plays Sam Winchester on *Supernatural.* Points for popularity. And the goblin hair.

Naming your kid Jar-Jar after the most reviled *Star Wars* protagonist ever doesn't seem like the way to go. It really doesn't.

Jasmine was obviously popularized by *Aladdin,* and may result in offers to "show you the world." Jasmine "Jaz" Anderson is a young ice magician in Rick Riordan's *The Kane Chronicles* and Jasmine Dubrow is the hero's love interest in *Independence Day.* The related Yasmin and Yasmine are other Jasmine variations.

Jessamine (from jasmine) was used in Britain around

1900, along with other flower-related names. Jessamine Lovelace is a troubled character in *The Infernal Devices* series, while Jessamine Wentworth is one of 12 sisters in Heather Dixon's fairytale novel *Entwined.* It's a bit old fashioned and literally quite flowery.

Jason is a hero in *Percy Jackson,* named for the hero of Greek myth. Jason Stackhouse is a lead on *True Blood,* as the heroine's hapless but heroic brother. Another scares viewers in *Friday the 13th*. Jaxom from Anne McCaffrey's *The Dragonriders of Pern* seems like a choice as a Jason variant, while the X makes it sound science-fictional.

On *Firefly,* Jayne has a gender-swapped name. This is ironic as he is the most brutish, crudest character. Jayne's name may be a portmanteau or squashing-together of John Wayne. Historically, it's actually derived from the English surname Jayne from Worcester. As such, it's a patronym of Jan, which comes from John. There's also Jaena, Han and Leia's daughter in the expanded *Star Wars* novel universe and the Wonder Twins, Zan and Jayna. See John, Jane

Jean Grey may be the only X-Man without a cool codename. While this is the English feminine variant, it's most common as the (male) French take on John. Heading up science fiction is Jean-Luc Picard. Jean-Claude is a vampire main character in the *Anita Blake* books, while Jean Passepartout is the long-suffering manservant in *Around the World in Eighty Days.* Jean Piaget was the most important figure in the 20th-century developmental psychology, particularly concerned with understanding in children. Jean-Baptiste Lamarck was a legendary French biologist interested in genetics. Make it so!

If you're a J.J. Abrams fan, then Jeffery (for Jeffrey Jacob Abrams) may prove a fun namesake. There's also

Jeffrey Spender, an FBI character from *The X-Files*, Jeff from *The Maze Runner*, and Jeffrey Sinclair, brooding commander of *Babylon 5*. The name means "God's peace." To be fair, the kid won't be too harassed this way and may in fact get that peace.

Jennifer, the most popular American eighties name, is surprisingly rare in science fiction. *Star Trek* brings us the captain's wife Jennifer Sisko and Jennifer Lien (who played Kes). Jennifer Walters is She-Hulk. *Buffy* has mysterious techno-pagan Jenny Calendar, and *Doctor Who,* the heroic girlfriend of Madame Vastra, Victorian lesbian crimefighting heroine. There's Jen the Gelfling from *The Dark Crystal,* Jenna Sommers of *The Vampire Diaries,* and Jenna, heroine of Jane Yolen's *Sister Light, Sister Dark*. The name is actually a variant on Guinevere, "fair one" (Which is certainly fantastical if rather obvious in its origins). Jennifer Lowell is Guinevere reborn in *The Fionavar Tapestry*. Variants on this include Gwen Cooper from *Torchwood* and Ginny Weasley from *Harry Potter.* A male adaptation could be Jensen Ackles who plays Dean Winchester. Nice spectrum, nice superpowers.

Jeor Mormont's name was invented by the *Game of Thrones* author. Presumably it's adapted from George and probably should be adapted back, for the non-Norman warriors.

Jeremy comes from Jeremiah, meaning "God uplifts." While the *Outlander* characters name for the latter, the former is much more modern. Jeremy Clockson is a hero in Terry Pratchett's *Discworld.* There's Jeremy Gilbert of *The Vampire Diaries.* Jeremy Hilary Boob is the "nowhere man" from The Beatles' film, *Yellow Submarine.*

Jeri Ryan (from Geraldine, "spear rule") plays Seven of Nine, likely cast for how hot she looks in her catsuit. Is that really your naming criteria? See Gerald.

Jessica Merriam Drew is the real name of Spider-Woman, while Jessica "Jesse" Miriam Reeves is a vampire in Anne Rice's *The Vampire Chronicles.* Your own Jessica Miriam might or might not find this cute. Marvel's Jessica Jones now has her own TV show (she's tough but chillingly ruthless in this Marvel superhero story *not* for kids). Jessica Hamby is the sexy though oh-so innocent redhead vampire on *True Blood.* Jessie is also a *Pokémon* character. And don't forget Disney star Jessica Rabbit (is there a reason all the Jessicas are sexy, vampires, or sexy vampires, all in slinky outfits?). Of course, they're not all bad, they're just drawn that way. The name, incredibly popular in the eighties, was invented by Shakespeare for *Merchant of Venice* (giving it a geeky origin in itself) and likely meaning foresight (also geeky in itself – wow). Five happy babies, but you may risk having the kid get a disturbing bite on reaching the gorgeous years.

Jet is the rebel outlaw in *Avatar* and a young lord in Jane Lindeskold's fantasy books. Presumably they are named for the mineral, not the plane, though you can tell yourself what you wish…

Jewel Staite (Kaylee) must have some devoted *Firefly* namesakes, though the name sounds fictitious from the first. Jewel is also a unicorn and close friend of Tirian in the C.S. Lewis books. There's also a Marvel superheroine, aka Jessica Jones.

Jill Pole is a heroine from the Narnia adventures, though the name appears surprisingly rare in the SF world. A few more appear in *Vampire Academy*, the *Resident Evil* video game series, and the *Scream* movies. It's a varient on Julia, "youthful," but may result in lots of climbing hills.

Jim see James

Jisa is a heroine queen in Mercedes Lackey's Valdemar books. It's jist a little strange, but certainly *could* be a name. If we need another "J name" in English. Her buddy Jisbella McQueen is a clever criminal in the novel *The Stars my Destination*

Joanne is JK Rowling's real name if you're a big Potter fan or hoping for a little author. For superpowers, Joanne Collins appears in *Heroes Reborn,* and Joanna Cargill is Frenzy of the X-Men. There's science fiction author Joanna Russ, and more in *Witches of East End, The Return,* and CW's *Supernatural.* Joanne is the mother of *Mirrormask.* Obscure but powerful in scifi. See Johanna

Jocelyn is the mother in *The Mortal Instruments.* Her name comes from "lord." British astrophysicist Jocelyn Bell Burnell is famous for her discovery of the first radio pulsars. Joscelin Verreuil is the greatest warrior in the *Kushiel* series by Jacqueline Carey. Something of a girly name if you're not French. Or maybe if you are.

Joe see Joseph

Joffrey is a little s**t in *Game of Thrones.* Possibly the worst character there is. Plus, dead. Good riddance.

Johanna Mason is a tough girl in *The Hunger Games* while Johanna Constantine is an 18th-century supernatural adventuress in *The Sandman.* The name means "grace of God." On the flip side, Johan Liebert of the anime *Monster* is a serial killer often called the greatest villain in anime history. Johannes Kepler was a key player in the scientific revolution, while Johannes Gutenberg, inventor of the printing press, changed the world of books forever. Apparently big changes surround this one.

"Heeeeere's Johnny!" John/Jonathan/Joan is the most popular name in the world (also see Jane, Jean, Joanne, Johanna, Ian). Johns are the hero of *Babylon 5, Stargate* (as Jack), *Farscape*, *Minority Report,* and *Star Trek* (as Jean-Luc Picard and Jonathan Archer). Though the writers seem to like "everyman names," as in the hero of *Brave New World* or Sherlock Holmes's sidekick, your child may be preparing for captaincy. As this universal name, it's popular in folk and fairytales with Trusty John (Faithful Johannes); Iron John; John Henry, Jack the Giant-Killer, Jack and Jill, Jack Hormer, and the beanstalk one. John Dee, also known as Doctor Destiny, is a DC Comics villain named from history. John Constantine is a con man and magician in Neil Gaiman's *The Sandman* as well as in his own line.

Science fiction has John Carter of Mars, DC's J'onn J'onnz, Jonathan Kent – Superman's father – John Winchester (*Supernatural*), and John Locke (*Lost*). Jonathan is a villain and hero in *The Mortal Instruments,* while Prince Jonathan of Conte is a hero and love interest of Tamora Pierce's books. There's John Doggett from *The X-Files* and Jonathan Levinson, something of a wimp on *Buffy*. Jonathan Doors tries to save humanity from the aliens in *Earth: Final Conflict.* Jon Snow is a hero of *Game of Thrones,* named for noble Jon Arryn. Robin Hood features Prince John and Little John. John is Wendy's brother in *Peter Pan.*

Actors include Jonathan Frakes, John Barrowman, John Billingsley (Phlox), Jon Pertwee (Third Doctor), John Cleese, John Hurt (*Merlin, Doctor Who*) and John Rhys-Davies. There are astronauts John Glenn, Jack Swigert, and John Young. Joan Higginbotham was an astronaut on STS-116. Authors include Tolkien – how can it get geekier? Plus John Brunner and Jonathan Swift. John Archibald Wheeler is responsible for the popularization of the term "black hole" and coining terms such as "wormhole." Famed mathematician John Napier created logarithm tables.

More variants include *Firefly*'s Jayne Cobb and *Alien Resurrection*'s Johner. Joan Dale Trevor was Miss America, a Golden Age comic book heroine, and Joan Watson gender flips Sherlock Holmes's friend on *Elementary*. In "Tabula Rasa," Buffy names herself Joan, for Joan of Arc.

Jolene Blalock plays T'Pol…and Jolene probably makes a better namesake. T'Pol sounds Vulcan and it sounds like topple.

Jonah "dove" has several namesakes. Jonas is the Vision of the *Young Avengers*. There's Jonas, the eleven-year-old protagonist of *The Giver*. Jonah Woodson Hex, a western comic book antihero, and J. Jonah Jameson, Spider-Man's editor. The latter is more volatile than peaceful.

Sir Jorah Mormont is kind of the sad sack of Westeros and never gets the girl. Plus, it smacks of high fantasy.

Joseph "may God increase" is a Bible hero, and also the birth name of Joseph Hill "Joss" Whedon. In the sciences, Joseph Lister invented a powerful antiseptic. Joseph Priestley was an English scientist, philosopher, and theologian with more than 150 publications. There's also science fiction author Joe Haldeman. Grandpa Joe is a beloved hero in *Charlie and the Chocolate Factory,* if a bit elderly. Josephine "Jo" Grant was a goofy *Doctor Who* companion. Watch the clumsiness and world-hopping.

Joshamee is the first name of Mr. Gibbs from *Pirates of the Caribbean*. A search online turns up all pirate references, suggesting the moviemakers invented it.

Joss Whedon self-named, and his name is Chinese for lucky.

Joxer is Xena's sidekick. It sounds made-up and adapted from jester or jokester. Don't make your kid the family joke.

Joyce Summers is Buffy's mother. Joyce is derived from "Josse," meaning "lord."

Jubilation Lee is the real name of X-Man Jubilee. A Southern name…somehow I though the Confederacy was gone by now.

Judith Resnik was an astronaut who died on the Challenger. In the Bible, she's a tough heroine who decapitates the villain. Meaning "She will be praised," she gives her name to the gentle Judy Jetson.

Meaning "Jove's child, or youthful," Julian appears as the doctor in *Deep Space Nine,* Julian Luthor, Lex Luthor's brother in the TV series *Smallville,* a prince of Amber, and Julian Blackthorn, a teen hero in *The Dark Artifices* by Cassandra Clare. Jules Verne would distinguish any name, especially now in the Steampunk era. Julius Kane is hero kids Carter and Sadie's father in Rick Riordan's *The Kane Chronicles. Independence Day* stars Judd Hirsch as the hero's father, Julius Levinson

Juliet Capulet, the protagonist in Shakespeare's tragedy, *Romeo & Juliet* has really set the standard for her namesakes. Juliet Stollop is a romantic heroine in Terry Pratchett's Discworld – she's actually reenacting Romeo and Juliet in her star-crossed love. There's Juliet Burke on *Lost* and Juliet Van Heusen on *Wizards of Waverly Place.* Juliet Landau plays vampires Drusilla on *Buffy.* Julia is Winston's multifaceted lover in *1984,* while Juliet Butler is the clever sister of Artemis Fowl's bodyguard. Julie "Lightspeed" Power is a young superheroine in *Power*

Pack. Julie Payette of Canada was an astronaut on STS-96, STS-127.

Kage Warriors star in *The Clone Wars*. Since 2008, there was a surge in Kage as a boy's name. 84 were born in 2014, compared to 54 in 2007 (Holeman).

Kahlan is the butt-kicking heroine of Terry Goodkind's *Sword of Truth* series. Seems like an odd spelling of Kaylyn to me. Plus no one can pronounce it.

Hawaiian for "the heavens," Kalani is a super tactical droid during the Clone Wars.

Maz Kanata, ambiguous pirate in *Star Wars VII*, has a second name that's Mohawk for village. It could work in English, though.

"Khaaaaan!" No.

Kara see Cara

Karathanelan Jadrevalyn is a prince in Mercedes Lackey's Valdemar books. He prefers the gallant "Karath" to the dorky "Thanel." Why don't you skip them both.

Karen Nyberg was an astronaut on STS-124 and Soyuz TMA-09M. Keren is a butt-kicking heroine in Mercedes Lackey's Valdemar books. Karrin Murphy works with Dresden in The *Dresden Files*. Karen Page is Daredevil's girlfriend and Karen Starr is an alias of Power Girl. The latter comes from her real name Kara, but using this name may ensure a young superheroine. It's all short for Katherine, "pure."

Karl see Carl

Katherine/Cathy/Kate/Catelyn appears throughout spec fic and fandom. On *Buffy* and *Angel* there's Katrina ("Dead Things"), Kate Lockley, Kathy Newman, and Kitty Fantastico. Kaylee stars in *Firefly*. Kate Beckett stars on *Castle*. The love interest of *Babylon 5* is Catherine Sakai

Katherine Pulaski (Next Generation) and Kate Mulgrew (playing Kathryn Janeway) rule *Star Trek*. Katherine Murry is the beloved mother in A *Wrinkle in Time*. Catherine stars in *Beauty and the Beast* and its remake. There's Katherine Pierce of *The Vampire Diaries*.

In the superhero world, Katherine Anne "Kitty" Pride is one of the most beloved X-Men, Shadowcat, though Katie Power is honorary X-Man Energizer. Kate Bishop is the new Hawkeye of the Young Avengers. Katherine Rebecca "Kate" Kane is Batwoman. Kat Farrell is a Marvel Universe reporter and there's also Manhunter (Kate Spencer).

There's Catelyn Stark of *Game of Thrones* and Cate Blanchett (Galadriel). Kat (*Being Human* US), Kate Austen (*Lost*), Katie Bell (*Harry Potter*, Gryffindor Chaser). Katarina was nearly the shortest-lived *Doctor Who* companion. Kathryn Nolan is the alternate form of Princess Abigail in *Once Upon a Time*. Many Irish princesses in folklore and balladry are called Kathleen (J.K. Rowling's middle name). There are also characters called this on *Medium* and *Casper the Friendly Ghost*.

Kathryn Hire, Kathryn Sullivan, Catherine Coleman, and Kathryn Thornton were all astronauts. American scientist, Katharine Burr Blodgett is known for numerous important contributions to the field of industrial chemistry. Kate Vernon plays Ellen Tigh on new *Battlestar Galactica* and Katee Sackhoff plays Starbuck. Katie McGrath is Morgana on *Merlin*. Trina Robbins wrote the first all-women comic in the seventies. See Carl, Karen

"Katniss" is of course the cattail root, as she tells us. It's a food plant as nourishing as a potato, and she becomes the feeder and savior of her community. She's a butt-kicking heroine, though her namesake can be found floating in a pond.

Kaye (often a British short form of Katherine, "pure") is the heroine of Holly Black's beloved *Fairie Court* series. Kay was originally King Arthur's squire and Little Kay stars in Hans Christian Andersen's fairy tale "The Snow Queen." Kai is the handsome and clever prince in Marissa Meyer's fairytale series. Do consider whether the kid will spend his/her life listening to the jingle from Kay Jewelers, "Every kiss begins with Kay."

"Kaylee" Kaywinnit Lee Frye from *Firefly* has a fun nickname and a whimsical exotic formal name. She's perky. "You manage to find the bright side to every single thing," Simon tells her in "The Message" (F1.12). In English, Kaylee is sometimes a hyphenate of Kay and Lee (meaning meadow). The name is also an American variant on Kayla, Arabic and Hebrew for "laurel" or "crown." In Irish a céilidh (pronounced kaylee) is a celebration or dance party.

Kazul king of the dragons in Patricia C. Wrede's *Enchanted Forest Chronicles* likely has a better dragon name than human one.

K'Ehleyr has a Klingon name no teacher will ever spell. They'll be klueless.

Keladry is a girl-knight heroine of Tamora Pierce's books. Non-middle ages parents might update this to Kelly.

Kelirehenna (Keli) is a heroine in Terry Pratchett's Discworld. Clearly she doesn't like being called Kelirehenna. Neither will your kid.

Kelsier is a hero of Brandon Sanderson's *Mistborn,* the ultimate thief and escape artist. Still sounds like a programming language.

Kendra is Anglo-Saxon for prophetess (a fantasy name from the start). Kendra Young is an early season slayer in *Buffy*, while Kendra Saunders is DC's Hawkgirl. Kendra Dumbledore is the Muggleborn mother of Albus Dumbledore.

"Oh, my God! They killed Kenny!" T. Kenneth Mattingly II was an astronaut on Apollo 16, and there's a Kenny in *Being Human* US. The ill-fated Kenny stars on *South Park*. Kenneth is Scottish for handsome.

Kerowyn is a heroine in Mercedes Lackey's Valdemar books. She's an amazing warrior-heroine, but this one still looks hard to spell. It certainly *could* be a name…

Kes: Her people only live nine years on *Star Trek: Voyager*. Seems like a bad omen.

Kethry is a heroine in Mercedes Lackey's Valdemar books (Kerowyn's grandmother and a heroine-mage). Once again, this *could* be a name.

Kevin means handsome. Kevins appear in *Sin City,* among the X-Men (Changeling), on *Supernatural,* in *Tron,* and on *Up*. Kevin Laine is a bright, charming hero in *The Fionavar Tapestry*. One Kevin is "The Merlin" in *The Mists of Avalon*. Actor Kevin Sorbo stars in *Hercules* and *Andromeda*, for scifi-fantasy versatility. There's also scifi author Kevin J. Anderson.

Khairelikoblepharehglukumeilichephreidosd'enagouni, nicknamed Fred by Kit, is a white hole in *So You Want to*

Be a Wizard in the *Young Wizards* series. Or you could just rest your elbow on the keyboard.

Khaleesi is Daenerys's title on *Game of Thrones*. Still it seems to have caught on, probably among the show-only fans.

Kiera Swan, space pirate and bounty hunter in the *Star Wars* universe, broke into the top 300 most common female names in 2007. Nearly 500 girls were named Kiera in 2014 (Holeman). Kira appears in *Star Trek: Deep Space Nine* (as a last name), in *Death Note,* and in *Orphan Black.* There's also Kira the Gelfling from *The Dark Crystal.* This is the feminine form of the Irish Gaelic Kieran, "dusky or dark-haired."

Kili is a dwarf in *The Hobbit.* In the film, he's the hottest one, with the love story. Keeli is a *Star Wars* Clone Trooper captain and Kelly is a modern alternative, for either gender. It means "war," fittingly enough.

Kimberly Ford is the introspective seer of *The Fionavar Tapestry.* Her name means "from the wood of the royal forest." Seems appropriate for a human swept on a fantasy adventure. Likewise, Kimberly Hart is a Mighty Morphin Power Ranger.

Klaus Baudelaire is a main kid-hero character of Lemony Snicket's *A Series of Unfortunate Events.* He's also the wisecracking fish on *American Dad.* Klaus Wulfenbach is a baron in *Girl Genius,* though something of a villain. Watch out for Santa Claus jokes.

Kosh is the enigmatic alien of *Babylon 5,* whose name sounds like a sneeze noise. It really does.

Korben, Bruce Willis' character who saves the

universe in *The Fifth Element,* sounds like a classic made up fictional name. Two sad babies.

Kurt Wagner is the real name of X-Man Nightcrawler, while Kurt Vonnegut, Jr was a truly innovative voice in science fiction. Thought it sounds curt, it actually means "courteous."

Kvothe is the protagonist of Patrick Rothfuss's *The Kingkiller Chronicle.* He's a dazzling hero who's done amazing things, but it really sounds like Quoth. On that note, Quoth the Raven in Discworld has one of the most awesome names, but you still shouldn't.

Kyle Rayner is Green Lantern, while Kyle Katarn appears in the game *Star Wars: Dark Forces.* It's Scottish for a narrow spit of land. Kyle Trager is the main character on TV's *Kyle XY.* There are more Kyles on *South Park, The Terminator* movies, the film *Beastly* and the video game *Dying Light.*

Strong with the Force and aggressive, Kylo Ren wields a unique lightsaber along with a quick temper. *The Force Awakens* was announced in 2012; by 2014 eight boys were named Kylo (Holeman). Kyle is a logical variant, though he may have the least evil name of any villain.

L from *Death Note* is a junk-food-eating oddball and master detective – the nerdy hero in opposition to Light, the sociopathic villain. Of course, everyone will think it's short for something. Maybe it is.

Lacy Rand is the best friend on *Caprica* with another in Riordan's books. It means "from Lassy" rather than "covered in lace."

Lafayette Reynolds is a sassy character on *True Blood.*

A fun character with a very French name.

Lana Lang is Clark Kent's girlfriend for a time and a main character on *Smallville*. Other Lanas appear in Michael Grant's *Gone* series, on the TV show *American Horror Story: Asylum* and as a friend in *The Princess Diaries*. The name is a variant on Alan, "little rock." Queen Lavana is the villainess of Marissa Meyer's fairytale series

Lancelot is the adulterous hero of the King Arthur stories. You might do better with Lance – *Pokémon* character and Marvel hero on *Agents of SHIELD*.

Landen Parke-Laine is the love interest of the *Thursday Next* series. His name ("long hill") seems awfully pretentious, even just the first one. Better than Thursday Next though.

Lando Calrissian and Londo Mollari both have alien names. And they're both traitors. What does this tell you? "Although just four boys were named Lando in 2014, the name reached its peak of popularity with 25 in 1980 – the year *The Empire Strikes Back* introduced Lando Calrissian to the world" (Holeman).

Lara ("citadel") is Superman's mother and a smoother choice than Jor-El. Of course, this was popularized by Lara Antipova from *Doctor Zhivago* with the beloved music "Lara's Theme." Hey, a kid with built-in theme music is quite appropriately geeky! Lara Croft of *Tomb Raider* has also made a name for herself with her, um, figure.

Lark, with thread magic, is a magical teacher at Winding Circle in *Circle of Magic*. She's named for the bird, but there are more standard bird names out there. Take Dodo, for instance.

Larry Niven is the author of the *Ringworld* series, while a "Larry Stu" occurs when a young writer creates a perfect character much like himself. No telling which kind of author you'll get. There's also Larry LaSalle, a villain in *Heroes,* and Larry the Lobster from *SpongeBob SquarePants.* The name is short for Laurence, "from Laurentium."

Laura Kinney is X-23 of the X-Men (now Wolverine), while Laura Roslin is the beloved and courageous president on new *Battlestar Galactica.* Laurel B. Clark, M.D. was an astronaut on STS-107. She died on the crash of the Columbia. Laurel is also a heroine in Mercedes Lackey's *Valdemar* books, and the real name of Black Canary on *Arrow. Men in Black* stars Laurel Weaver as Agent L. Dr. Lora Baines appears in *Tron.* The name means the laurel tree. Five happy babies, or four if you know the Greek myth of Daphne.

From Roald Dahl's *Matilda* and from *Harry Potter,* Lavender is a seldom used floral name. You seem to be setting up her color preferences in advance.

Lebannen, King of Earthsea certainly has an impressive secret name, meaning "rowan tree" in the Old Speech, according to the book. He's called something more normal, which might be a good way to go.

Lee is the pilot Apollo on new *Battlestar Galactica.* Also a Hogwarts Quidditch commentator and a hero of the *His Dark Materials* series. Lee Fletcher hails from Riordan's books, Dr. Lee Rosen is a main character from TV's *Alphas,* and Lee Everett stars in *The Walking Dead* video game. This is Kaylee's middle name on *Firefly.* Lee means shelter or protection, sometimes meadow.

Leela is a butt-kicking savage on *Futurama* and another one on *Doctor Who.* Leela smash! Best strengthen the furniture now. Leeta, possibly a variant, is a hostess at Quark's on *Deep Space Nine*. There's also a telepath named Lyta in *Babylon 5*. And there's Leeloo, a divine being sent to save the universe in *The Fifth Element*.

Legolas Greenleaf under the tree, you're a sixties flower child, between you and me.

Leia matches the Hebrew pronunciation of Leah, meaning weary (a problematic meaning, I'd say). In Hawaiian Leia is "Child of heaven; heavenly flowers." Much nicer. Although this name surged when the original *Star Wars* film was released in 1977, the name has greatly increased much more recently with 605 baby girls named Leia in 2014 (Holeman). Still identifiable.

Lelouch Lamperouge from the anime *Code Geass* is a maniacal and murderous mastermind who began as a hero but slowly turned despot. A warning for us all.

Lemony Snicket was a goofy author name made up on the spot by Daniel Handler. Your kid may have sour feelings…

Leonard McCoy and Leonard Nimoy defined *Star Trek*. Leonard from *Big Bang Theory* may be named in homage. The meaning of the name Leopold is "Bold people" or possibly lion. Leopold is the father of Snow White in *Once Upon a Time*. Leon S. Kennedy appears in the game *Resident Evil*. Of course, Leonardo da Vinci gave his name to many characters, including a Ninja Turtle and the star of *DaVinci's Demons*. Leo is a hero in *Percy Jackson* and Leonid is a young Russian magician in Riordan's *The Kane Chronicles*. Leopold "Leo" Fitz stars on *Agents of SHIELD*. Finally, Leonard of Quirm is a parody of Leonardo da Vinci in Terry Pratchett's Discworld.

Lessa is a character in Anne McCaffrey's *The Dragonriders of Pern.* Is she looking for Greata?

Lestat de Lioncourt is a hero of Anne Rice's *The Vampire Chronicles.* And, y'know, a creepy vampire.

Liam Kinkade is the hero of the show *Earth: Final Conflict.* It's also Angel the vampire's real name and a character in *Being Human* (US). Liam Hemsworth plays Gale in *The Hunger Games.* Liam Neeson appeared in the new *Star Wars* and other popular films. A variant on William, it means protector. It's #1 in 2015, probably for the movie stars.

Liessa Dragonlady is a heroine in Terry Pratchett's Discworld. If you name the kid this, you're probably predetermining her path.

In *Death Note,* Light Yagami is diabolical and calculating, despite his shining name. This just proves, names can flip on you!

Lilah (Hebrew for "night") is frequently a liar, emphasized by the first syllable of her name. The series bad girl also references this concept on *Angel:* WESLEY: It's a lie! LILAH: Lah. It's a Lilah. Delilah from Jennifer Roberson's *Tiger and Del* novels has an equally unfortunate name, but she shortens it.

Lilith was Adam's first wife according to some interpretations of the Bible. In Jewish lore, she became a demon and was only reclaimed in recent decades as a model of feminist empowerment. She stood for a rejection of traditional marriage and family life. Lilith Sternin, the character on *Cheers* and *Frasier,* represents this naming trend. The name is most often seen in fantasy series as a demon on *Supernatural, True Blood,* and the video game *Borderlands* and in the *Nevermore* book series by Kelly Creagh and the *Mortal Instruments* series by Cassandra Clare. Also, superheroine Lilith Clay occasionally appears in DC Comic's *Teen Titans* titles. This is Girl Genius's adoptive mother.

Lily Potter is Harry Potter's heroic, self-sacrificing mother, murdered by Lord Voldemort. This name goes to the actress in *Mortal Instruments* and Lily Munster, the vampire wife in the show *The Munsters.* Lily is Jonas's little sister in *The Giver,* and Lilit is the heroine of *Legend.* This name goes to princesses in *Entwined* by Heather Dixon and *Princess of the Midnight Ball.* While lilies seem pure, pacifist flowers, Lily Sloane is an action heroine in *Star Trek: First Contact* and Lili Marquette is one in of *Earth: Final Conflict.* #14 in 2015.

Linda Danvers is Supergirl and Linda Godwin was an astronaut on STS-37, STS-59, STS-76, STS-108. Despite her many missions, Linda ("pretty") doesn't seem to have caught on in scifi.

Lindsey is more often a girl's name than a boy's. Lindsay Weir is a character on TV's *Freaks & Geeks.* Lindsey McDonald is an evil lawyer on *Angel* who gets an evil hand and falls for a bloodsucking vampire, among other tragedies. His name means "island of linden trees."

Lír is a hero-prince in *The Last Unicorn.* Odd that his father King Haggard couldn't afford more syllables. In Gaelic myth, the Children of Lir are transformed into swans. Liir may be Elphaba's son in *Wicked.* Seems like a royalty thing, especially for dithering, uncertain princes.

Lirael is Abhorsen-in-Waiting in Garth Nix's series. It's a lovely lyrical name, if fictional.

Llewella ("shining one"), princess of Amber in *The Chronicles of Amber* has an incredibly Welsh name.

Lloyd Alexander, author of the *Chronicles of Prydain,* adds distinction to this name. Originating with the Welsh adjective llwyd, it means "grey." Lloyds star in the films *Say Anything* and *Dumb and Dumber,* as well as the animated series *Lloyd in Space* and *Ninjago: Masters of Spinjitzu.*

James "Logan" Howlett, Wolverine of *X-Men*, is a manly man and one of the top superheroes. There were also attractive guys named Logan in *The Babysitter's Club,* and on *Dark Angel, Zoey 101, Veronica Mars* and *Gilmore Girls.* It's a Scottish last name that once meant hollow, if the meaning could do anything to deter you from this butt-kicking homage. #5 in 2015.

Lois Lane has varied through the eras of *Superman,* but she's often been an opinionated action heroine. Suitably, her name means "most desirable." There's also top authors Lois Lowry and Lois McMaster Bujold. For empowerment geeks, Lois Weber was the first woman to direct a full-length feature film.

Evil Norse god Loki is seen in *The Avengers* franchise and in *The Sandman* comics, like Odin. Perhaps this one will catch on and we will have many loci of Loki.

Loonquawl received Deep Thought's answer to Life, the Universe, and Everything. However he received no answer on why someone was cruel enough to name him Loonquawl. Perhaps the name leads to philosophizing.

Lorien is a forest and god in *Lord of the Rings* and an old wizardly guy on *Babylon 5.* It certainly sounds like a peaceful forest. And maybe a name. Maybe not. Two sad babies for the uncertainty of it all. There's a Lorin in

Shannara. With a similar name, Loren Silvercloak, and his source Matt Sören, star in *The Fionavar Tapestry.*

Lorne means "forsaken," which certainly seems a gloomy choice for a name meaning. Canadian actor Lorne Greene was the original Captain Adama, Lorna Dane is Polaris of the X-Men while Lorena Marquez is Aquagirl. On *Angel,* there's friendly lounge-singing demon Lorne – really Krevlorneswath of the Deathwok Clan. Admittedly, this would be worse.

Louis Pasteur invented pasteurization, while Louis Latimer was a famous American inventor. There's Luís Ponce de León, explorer and often fictional character. Another is Dr. Louise Colubra – the Murry family doctor in Madeleine L'Engle's books, with the namesake of Louise the Larger, a telepathic snake. Louis de Pointe du Lac hails from Anne Rice's *The Vampire Chronicles.* It means "renowned warrior" and could work for C.S. Lewis too. And let's not forget Lewis Carroll (pseudonym of Charles Lutwidge Dodgson), author of *Alice in Wonderland.*

Lucas see Luke

Lucian means light, coming from the same roots as Lucifer. Thus it works well for the fallen angel type…though three sad babies suggest it's obscure and subtly evil sounding. Though you could call him Luke of course. Namesakes include a lycan from the movie *Underworld,* a heroic werewolf in Cassandra Clare's young adult series *The Mortal Instruments,* an Imperial assassin in *The Elder Scrolls* and the Cahill family in the *39 Clues* series. Lucien is also the chief librarian in The Dreaming, seen in the *Sandman* comics. Lucius Malfoy certainly adds villainy points, though Lucius Tadius da Lucca is a hero in the *Kushiel* series by Jacqueline Carey and Lucivar Yaslana is a demonic hero in *The Black Jewels Trilogy.* See Luke

Lucifer is the ruler and then former ruler of Hell, a charming, intelligent, and utterly ruthless fallen angel. He's seen in *Sandman* comics, on *Supernatural,* and in the *Dark Jewels* trilogy and in the *Ink and Steel* series by Elizabeth Bear as well as his eponymous comic and upcoming TV series on Fox. Classmates may be tempted to talk to him in a Ricky Ricardo accent.

Lucrezia, matriarch of *Girl Genius,* has a name that's thought to come from the Latin lucrum, meaning "profit, wealth." An optimistic wish for the future, though she may turn out greedy. There's also Lucrezia Noin from the anime *Mobile Suit Gundam Wing* and Lucrezia Smith in Virginia Woolf's novel *Mrs Dalloway.* Lucrezia Borgia, illegitimate daughter of Pope Alexander VI, stars in *The Borgias,* of course.

Lucy, "light," is a delightful name. The Narnia heroine is the obvious reference, though Lucy is Dracula's first victim. Equally tragic, she's the wife of Harold Saxon (the Master) in *Doctor Who* and the wife of Sweeney Todd. Percy Weasley names his daughter this, and Lois Lane has a sister called this. More appear in *The Big Bang Theory, Across the Universe, Septimus Heap,* and animes *Elfen Lied* and *Fairy Tail.* Plus the movie *Lucy,* of course. There's the Peanuts character. And don't forget *I Love Lucy.* Luciana Carro plays Louanne "Kat" Katraine on new *Battlestar Galactica.* More importantly, there's Lucy Lawless, who plays Xena and also appears on *Agents of SHIELD* and *Battlestar Galactica.*

Ludo also means light, though it sounds terribly lunky. Ludo Bagman is Head of Magical Games and Sports in the Ministry of Magic. He's an endearing monster on *Labyrinth* who befriends rocks. Really.

Luke Skywalker has a scifi name you can certainly get away with. The name comes from Lukas (man from Loucania) and is associated with the Biblical disciple, though the Lucian variant means light (and is related to Lucifer, fallen angel of light). In 2015, Lucas was #6 and Luke was #16. Luke/Lucian is a hero in *The Mortal Instruments*. Lucas Bishop is Bishop of the X-Men. Luke Castellan is a traitor in *Percy Jackson*. There's also a minor *Buffy* villain and Sarah Jane's genius son in the *Doctor Who* universe. Five happy babies plus scifi points.

Luminara Unduli is a Jedi Master, in *Star Wars Rebels*. With an exotic, fluffy, light-filled name.

Luna Lovegood stars in *Harry Potter,* though she's a bit loony and often called that (be warned). The series gave this name a big popularity jump of course. Luna appears in *Sailor Moon* and is a *My Little Pony*. The name means "moon" of course, giving viewers a hint that Luna Garza is a shapeshifting mom on *True Blood*. Also, Luna is Sailor Moon's talking black cat.

Lupin, "wolflike," traveled far and wide in search of treasure and women, reinventing anime as something for older viewers. Remus Lupin, *Harry Potter*'s werewolf, shares this name.

Lursa is a Klingon villainess in *ST: TNG*, who sounds like she goes lurching about. It's up there with Drizzella.

Lúthien was the fairest elf ever in Middle Earth. It could be a name…though it's not.

Lwaxana Troi has an alien name with some very alien letters, as the mother of Deanna Troi on *Next Generation*. She's also an annoying Auntie Mame figure.

Lydia Deetz hails from *Beetlejuice,* though she's very dark. Perhaps it's the pain of her last name… There's also Lydia Hadley, mother in Ray Bradbury's short story, "The Veldt" and Lydia Martin of *Teen Wolf.* Another appears in *The Walking Dead* comic books. The original "woman from Lydia" is a Bible character.

Lynne, "house," comes from Lynette of King Arthur's tales, handmaiden and advisor to the Lady of the Fountain. Evil-Lyn is a villain of *Masters of the Universe* with terrible pigmentation. See Linda

Lyra is a constellation name taken from the lyre of Orpheus, linking to music, astronomy, and mythology… though it also sounds like "liar," leading to playground taunts. Lyra Belacqua is the child heroine of Philip Pullman's series *The Golden Compass/His Dark Materials.* Lyra is also a young heroine in Mercedes Lackey's *Valdemar* books. Another is the new She-Hulk

Lyta Alexander is a telepath on *Babylon 5.* Somewhere between heroine and antiheroine, with a memorable sex scene you shouldn't show the kiddies. This may come from Hippolyta or Lolita.

In 2014, 61 boys were named Mace (Holeman). Mace Windu kicked butt in the *Star Wars* prequels of course. And it's a deadly weapon (actually two kinds of weapon). Often short for Mason.

Madeleine is a vampire in Anne Rice's *The Vampire Chronicles* series, though the name will always be linked with the children's series of *Madeline* picture books. Madeleine L'Engle (1918–2007), author of the Newberry winning *A Wrinkle in Time* before children's science fiction existed, lends style to any name. Madelyne Jennifer Pryor is the Red Queen, a clone of Jean Grey in *X-Men.* The name is related to Mary Magdalene. #10 in 2014.

Madmartigan, hero of *Willow,* has a name that's one in a million. Seriously. There shouldn't be two.

Magenta, the maid from *Rocky Horror,* may have been this color when she was born but this seems no reason to label her.

Magnus (great) is the name of *X-Men* Super-villain/heroes, Magneto aka Erik Magnus Lehnsherr. Magnus Bane is a hero in *The Mortal Instruments,* while another Magnus sired Anne Rice's vampire Lestat.

Maia is a werewolf heroine in *The Mortal Instruments.* She's named for the Titaness and mother of Hermes. Thumbelina is called this at the end of her original tale, and Maia Rutledge-Skoures appears on *The 4400.*

Majikthise and Vroomfondel may or may not be philosophers in *Hitchhiker's Guide.* The suitability of their names is less of a question.

Malcolm Reynolds, captain of Serenity, is a beloved scifi character, while Malcolm Reed runs the ship on *Enterprise.* Malcolm is also a vampire character in the *Anita Blake* books and an ambiguous character on *Arrow.* Malcolm Reynolds is called "Mal." River points out that in the Latin, Mal means "bad." He certainly prides himself on this with his iconic line, "I aim to misbehave." Malcolm actually means "devotee of St. Colomba" – the saint who preached to and converted much of Scotland.

Maleficent…villains get such terrible names. This one means "bad intentions." She did get a movie though.

Malina Bennet (Hebrew for "from the tower") is the

chosen one in *Heroes Reborn.*

Mara is a god in the *Belgariad,* while Mara Jade is something of an antiheroine in the *Star Wars* novels. Hebrew for bitter, it can be a Mary variant. Mara is also the name of Kang's wife on *Star Trek,* a demon in the manga and anime series *Oh My Goddess*! and heroine of the *Empire Trilogy* by Raymond E. Feist and Janny Wurts

Margaret (pearl) has many namesakes. *Game of Thrones* has Margaery Tyrell. There's Margaret "Meg" Murry in *A Wrinkle in Time* and the girl from *Are You There, God? It's me, Margaret.* Maggie Walsh is Buffy's no-nonsense mentor, a Margaret Thatcher figure. Madge Undersee and Mags from *The Hunger Games* are both concealed pearls – women with hidden value.

Authors include Margaret Atwood, Marge Piercy, and Margaret Cavendish (creator of the first utopian novel in the 17th century). Marguerite Perey discovered the chemical element francium in 1939.

Lt. Margaret "Racetrack" Edmondson is a pilot on new *Battlestar Galactica.* Witchy heroine Magrat Garlick in Terry Pratchett's Discworld has awkward spelling by mistake. Megan Gwynn is Pixie of the X-Men. Marguerite is the heroine of *The Scarlet Pimpernel,* one of the precursors of masked superhero fiction. Meggie Folchart is the child protagonist of *Inkheart.* A popular shortening is Peggy – Peggy Whitson was an astronaut and Peggy Carter, Captain America's love interest, now has her own show.

In Latin, Marcus means Hammer. Mark is a king in Arthurian legend. Marcus is a hero in *Babylon 5,* while Marcus "Augur" Deveraux is the tech genius of *Earth: Final Conflict.* Marcus Hamilton is an adversary on *Angel,* played by Adam Baldwin. Marcus hails from *Being Human* (US). There are several *Star Trek* actors with this name: Marc Alaimo (Gul Dukat), Mark Allen Shepherd (Morn), and Mark Lenard (original Sarek). For a gender-flip, Marcie Cooper was Harlequin (one of several). The name totally hits the scifi mark.

Martha is a Bible name, meaning lady. Martha Jones is a beloved *Doctor Who* companion. Martha Kent and Martha Rogers are the heroes' mothers, in *Superman* and *Castle* respectively. Martha Johansson, also known as No-Girl, is an X-Man.

Marvel: A District One Tribute and the traveling magician of in *The Wizard of Oz*. Also a nod to Marvel comics, Captain Marvel, Ms. Marvel, and Marvelman. Sounds kind of full of himself though…

Marvin the Paranoid Android in *Hitchhiker's Guide* is a delightful, if whiny namesake. Celtic for "lives by the sea." Maybe if he did, he would be less uptight. But more rusty.

Mary (bitter, wished-for child – these certainly seem like contradictions) may be the most popular name in Christian countries, with hundreds of variants like Maria and Marion. Certainly, there are plenty of namesakes for your geek child-to-be. First among these may be Mary Sue, the fanfiction stand-in for the author. But don't let that possibility stop you – Mary Sue Poots is also the name of *Agents of SHIELD* superheroine Skye. Other superheroes and superhero girlfriends include Mary Marvel, Mary Jane Watson, and Anna Marie (Rogue).

In classic literature you can see Maid Marian go on adventures (sometimes fighting ones, depending on the adaptation), while Sherlock Holmes' best friend Watson weds Mary Morstan. Children's books feature Mary Poppins. Rose Marion Tyler was the incredibly popular first companion in rebooted *Doctor Who,* while Maria Jackson is a child hero of *The Sarah Jane Adventures.* Authors include Mary Shelley, her mother Mary

Wollstonecraft, Marion Zimmer Bradley, and Alice Mary Norton (real name of Andre Norton). Maria Mitchell was the first female American professional astronomer, discovering a comet that was named for her. Mary L. Cleave and Mary Weber were astronauts too. Marie Curie would lend distinction to any name. Mary McDonnell plays President Roslin on new *Battlestar Galactica.* Mary Margaret is Snow White in *Once Upon a Time* and Mary Malone is a heroine of the *Golden Compass* series. There's Marie from the anime/manga *Soul Eater* and Marian Yaslana, a heroine in *The Black Jewels Trilogy.*

Maryann Forrester is the maenad antagonist of *True Blood.* In *Harry Potter,* there's the wimpy muggle-born Mary Cattermole, Marietta Edgecombe – a traitorous Ravenclaw student whom Hermione curses with magical acne, and Mary Riddle, grandmother of Voldemort (apparently, not J.K. Rowling's favorite name). There's Maureen "Muffy" Birnbaum, Barbarian Swordsperson. Marietta Cosmopilite is a precognizant heroine in Terry Pratchett's *Discworld.* Marina Sirtis plays Deanna Troy on *Star Trek,* and Marisa Coulter is the villain of *The Golden Compass.* Stelmaria, "star of the sea," is a familiar spirit there. Murray seems possible for a gender-flip. Also see Molly.

From Roald Dahl's *Matilda* comes a little supergenius with awesome mental powers. A lovely namesake, meaning battle-strength. That's cool too,

Between Matt Smith, the Eleventh Doctor, and Matt Murdock, Daredevil, this name has a running start. Matthew is a Biblical saint, whose name means "God's gift," though the name was Jewish before his arrival. There's also Matts on *Falling Skies, The Vampire Diaries,* and *Heroes,* in *The Fionavar Tapestry,* and captaining the Excalibur on *Babylon 5: Crusade.* Matrim (Mat) Cauthon is a hero in *The Wheel of Time.* Sir James Matthew Barrie is author of *Peter Pan.* Matthew is the raven companion of

Dream of the Endless in *Sandman.*

Max, "greatest," stars in *Dark Angel.* Max Grodénchik plays Rom on *Star Trek: Deep Space Nine.* Maxwell Lord is a DC comics villain. Max is a *Roswell* character and the hero of the *Mad Max* films. Dr. Max Patel stars in *Avatar.* Max Quordlepleen is an entertainer who hosts at Milliways, the Restaurant at the End of the Universe and the Big Bang Burger Bar. Another Max is the miracle worker in *The Princess Bride.* Despite all this the most popular may be the star of *Where the Wild Things Are.*

The English and Scottish name May references the month or may be short for Margaret, pearl. May is also another name for the hawthorn flower. Astronaut Mae Jameson is a memorable namesake. *The Hunger Games* offers Maysilee Donner, with a made-up name that may reference the month or its flower, the lily. She was Haymitch's partner in his own games, and Katniss inherits her monkingjay pin.

Maya Lopez is *Daredevil* superhero Echo. Hebrew for "water" or "illusion" in Sanskrit. A few appear in *Harvest Moon* and *Borderlands 2* video games. Maya was also the mythical mother of Hermes. My, that's a short list.

Medusa, the Greek demigoddess, has namesakes among the Marvel Inhumans and in the anime and manga series *Soul Eater.* Okay, snake-haired Greek monster so hideous she turns people to stone? That's gotta hit the top of cruel baby names, only below Jabba the Hutt.

Mekaneck is a heroic human periscope on *Masters of the Universe.* Only use if you want a small cyborg.

Melinda as a name hails from eighteenth century poetry, along with Belinda, Clarinda, Dorinda and

Florinda. Melinda Qiaolian "The Cavalry" May kicks butt with total discipline and control on *Agents of SHIELD.* Mel Bush, a *Doctor Who* companion, may be a namesake.

Melody Pond stars in new *Doctor Who* as the child of two companions and part Time Lord. Another is Ariel's daughter in *The Little Mermaid 2.* Superheroism guaranteed.

Mendanbar, King of the Enchanted Forest in Patricia C. Wrede's *Enchanted Forest Chronicles,* labors under an additional burden with his clunky, ponderous name.

Mera, Aquaman's love, clearly comes from the root "mar," sea. Meera Reed, warrior girl from *Game of Thrones,* could be another namesake, and for both, there's decent deniability. Four happy babies.

Mercedes Lackey is a popular fantasy author and there's also paranormal detective Mercy Thompson. The name is popularized by the true love of the Count of Monte Cristo, and is French for Mercy. However, the car company has complicated this. Two happy babies.

Meredith: The arrogant scientist of *Stargate Atlantis* Meredith Rodney McKay spends his life tortured by this girlie name, though it is still a masculine name today in Wales (just not anywhere else). Merriman Lyon, heroic Old One in *The Dark is Rising,* isn't particularly better (Merry Man? Really?) From the Welsh name Maredudd or Meredydd, possibly meaning "great lord" or "sea lord." Give a thought before you do this to a boy.

Meriadoc "Merry" Brandybuck: As with the other Tolkien names, everyone knows where it comes from. And naming a boy "Merry" seems cruel. A boy's name only Shel Silverstein or Johnny Cash could love.

Merida "one who has achieved high honor" is the first Pixar princess – a feisty, Scottish girl with wild red hair. Her name is actually a Spanish place name. In each of the two years since the 2012 release of *Brave,* more than 100 baby girls have been called Merida (Wolfers).

Merlin is King Arthur's wizard, with many namesakes in fantasy including Malcolm Merlyn from the DC universe and the television show *Arrow* and Merlin son of Corwin in *The Chronicles of Amber.* As a variant, Mervyn Pumpkinhead is Dream's cantankerous janitor in Neil Gaiman's *The Sandman.* Four sad babies, since everyone knows where you got this, and naming your kid this won't really make him a wizard.

Michael/Michelle certainly is a top American name with hundreds of references in the geeky world. A Biblical angel name meaning "Who is like God," it caught on in a way Zachroniel and Imriel really did not. #18 in 2015.

Science fiction gives us wisecracking security chief Michael Garibaldi of *Babylon 5* and Michael Dorn (Worf). Michael J. Fox starred in *Back to the Future,* and *Michael* is a John Travolta movie about an angel. Mike Yates was a Third Doctor companion. Michael Collins was Command Module Pilot on Apollo 11 and Michael J. Smith died on the Challenger. Michael Faraday, whose family was very poor, became one of the greatest scientists in history. Sarah Michelle Gellar played Buffy. Michael Rosenbaum plays Lex Luthor on *Smallville.* Mike Peterson is Deathlok on *Agents of SHIELD.* Michele Gonzales dates Spider-Man. Michelle Carter is a superhero in the DC Universe.

For kiddie novels, Michael is the name of the youngest child in both *Mary Poppins* and *Peter Pan,* while Michael Corner is Ginny Weasley and Cho Chang's boyfriend in *Harry Potter.* Mike Teavee is "a boy who does nothing but watch television" in *Charlie and the Chocolate Factory.*

The list keeps going with Michael Dawson (*Lost),* Mike

Wazowski (*Monsters Inc.*), Mike Nelson (*Mystery Science Theatre 3000*), Michael Samuelle (*La Femme Nikita*), Michael Glass (*Morganville Vampires*), Michael Vaughn (*Alias*), Michael Moscovitz (*The Princess Diaries*). Authors include Michael Crichton (*Jurassic Park,* etc.), Michael Stackpole, and J. Michael Straczynski (*Babylon 5*). Michael Hogan played Colonel Saul Tigh and Michael Trucco plays Samuel T. Anders on new *Battlestar Galactica.* Michael Palin was in *Monty Python.* Michelle Forbes played Ensign Ro (*ST: TNG*), Admiral Cain on *Battlestar Galactica,* and Retro Girl on *Powers.*

Mickey certainly leads people to the mouse, though Mickey Smith is a *Doctor Who* companion. Consider that this is traditionally short for Michael and go that route if you don't want a Mouseketeer.

Miles O'Brien of *Star Trek* is the clear association for Miles, meaning "merciful" or "soldier." There's Miles Straume (*Lost*), Miles from *Cars,* and Skye's hacker boyfriend off *Agents of SHIELD.* Colonel Miles Quaritch stars in *Avatar.* Myles of Olau is a kind mentor in Tamora Pierce's Tortall books. Milo stars in *Atlantis: The Lost Empire* and Meelo in *Avatar* is probably related. Be warned, "miles" is also a common American word, and if the *Cars* people picked up on the pun, kids will too.

Millicent Bulstrode is the only Slytherin student deemed nasty enough to date Draco. One assumes she was named this because the name sounds yucky. In a similar vein, Mildred is the unsympathetic wife in *Fahrenheit 451.* Millie is better – Millie Hughes-Fulford was an astronaut on STS-40 and *Millie the Model* is a Marvel comic. Millie is a character in *The Frog Princess* by E.D. Baker and in the *Warriors* series. Going the obscure route, this is also a pseudonym of George in *Dead Like Me.* Mildred is definitely out of fashion and even has a "dread" in it. In Latin Millie is "servant for the temple"; in English, "gentle strength." See Camilla.

Minerva? The Roman goddess of wisdom? Really? I guess you could call her Minnie… In *Harry Potter*, Minerva McGonagall is Deputy Headmistress of Hogwarts, and in the *Artemis Fowl* books, Minerva Paradizo is equally intellectual. Both are named for the Roman goddess of wisdom. Another Minerva is the kind landlady of Fenoglio in *Inkheart.* There's also a series of kids' mystery books centering on a Minerva Clark. Minerva Pott is a character in Dickens's novel. One sad baby.

Mina Harker is the heroine of *Dracula* – she comes out of the story human, though her counterpart in *League of Extraordinary Gentlemen* gets vamped into a superhero. Mina is German for "love" while Minna is Hebrew for "child of earth." Minnie Mouse has pretty much taken over, though Minnie was popular a century ago. Also works as a Japanese and Korean ethnic name (with a variety of meanings) or a Persian name meaning "azure."

Other namesakes include manga and anime Mina Carolina (*Attack on Titan),* Mina Tepeş (*Dance in the Vampire Bund*) and Mina Tsukishiro (*Getsumento Heiki Mina*). Mina Bonteri is a friend to Padmé Amidala in *Star Wars: The Clone Wars*, while Senator Meena Tills is the senator of Dac. She's a Mon Calamari, like Admiral Ackbar. Video games contribute Seong Mi-na (*Soul)* and Mina Majikina (*Samurai Shodown).* Be aware, there's also Mina Mongoose from *Sonic the Hedgehog.* See Wilhelmina

Minion is a name that definitely sets up a future of crank-winching or yellow skin and blue overalls. Menion Leah, the protagonist's friend in *The Sword of Shannara,* may be related.

Miranda is the heroine of *The Tempest,* Shakespeare's

sweet fantasy play with fairies and monsters. As such, there are many fantasy novels that play with the concept by naming their heroines this. Possibly in homage, Miranda Walker is a heroine in *The Sandman.* Miranda Leevald is Stacy X of the *X-Men.* Also Miranda Otto played Éowyn in the films.

Miriam doesn't seem to have a lot of namesakes, but Jessica Merriam Drew is Spider-Woman. See Mary.

Misty is a *Pokémon* character, or the nickname of author Mercedes Lackey. Also a famous horse.

Moirin "sea white" is a heroine in the *Kushiel* series by Jacqueline Carey. If you've read the book about her explicit adventures, you might shy away. Moiraine from *The Wheel of Time* may be related.

Moist is the sidekick of *Dr. Horrible.* Total drip. Also, Moist Von Lipwig is a hero in *Discworld.* Of course, the running joke is how terrible his name is. An excellent textbook example of parent brutality that your child can bring up at his emancipation hearing.

Molly Grue is a sharp-tongued everywoman heroine in *The Last Unicorn.* Molly Carpenter is Harry Dresden's apprentice in *The Dresden Files.* For superheroes, Molly Hayes is a strong superheroine in Marvel's *Runaways,* and the original Harlequin was Molly Mayne. Chief O'Brian of *Star Trek: DS9* names his kid this and Molly Weasley (née Prewett) is mother of Bill, Charlie, Percy, Fred, George, Ron and Ginny Weasley in *Harry Potter.* Of course, in recent times, Molly Hooper of *BBC Sherlock* is likely getting the most fan love. The name is a British variant on Mary (bitter), though it also means wished-for child (ah, much nicer than "bitter"). Five happy babies, plus bonus points for so many subtle sources across so much of scifi-fantasy.

The Childlike Empress of *The Neverending Story* gets a new name (that no one can make out) in the film. It's Moon Child. Pretty, but very flower child indeed.

Rollerball stars John Beck as Moonpie. This is also Sheldon Cooper's childhood nickname. Yet painful for saddling the kid with.

Mon Mothma is one of the few women in *Star Wars.* A powerful leader but her name resembles an alien insect.

Mordred is King Arthur's evil son. If that's the message you want to send, consider "Spawn of Satan" instead. *Babylon 5*'s villain Morden is likely a namesake as is the nasty Morfin Gaunt, uncle of Voldemort. Mordred Deschain in Stephen King's *Dark Tower* series is half human, half spider. Apparently that can happen…

Morgan le Fay is King Arthur's half-sister, usually a villain, though sometimes a protagonist sorceress (in *The Mists of Avalon* or *The Magic Treehouse* books, for instance). Her deliberately-chosen namesake Morgana appears in the show *Merlin*, Disney's *The Little Mermaid 2, Power Rangers, Darkwing Duck,* and *Wonder Woman.* The name possibly comes from the Morrigan, an Irish death goddess. However, *Enchanted* stars Morgan, the sweet six-year-old who still believes in magic. Variants include Morghann, a queen and heroine in *The Black Jewels Trilogy*; Morgase, the queen in *The Wheel of Time;* or Morwen, a practical witch in Wrede's *Enchanted Forest Chronicles.*

"Nanu-nanu," says Mork of *Mork & Mindy.* I know babies are alienlike, but really!

Morn is the alien barfly of *Star Trek: DS9.* You'll win

geeky trivia contests, but the kid may go into mourn-ing.

Mornelithe Falconsbane is a villain in Mercedes Lackey's Valdemar books. Just imagine your baby, little Mornelithe. It just sounds evil, doesn't it?

Mort means death, adding humor to Mort on Discworld. Mortimer, also meaning death, is a name that goes to the unfortunate *X-Men* villain Mortimer Toynbee, Toad. A rather stuffy and gloomy choice.

Mosquito from the anime and manga series *Soul Eater* is a bad choice. That's all. Also, Mosquitor is a *Masters of the Universe* villain. Really.

Mr. Mot is the alien barber on *Star Trek: The Next Generation*, if you're desperate for science fiction obscurity points. Warning: your kid may feel blue. Or look it.

Mundungus Fletcher is a sneak thief and antihero in *Harry Potter.* And people nickname him "dung." The same fate could befall your child...

Murray Bost Henson is "a journalist from one of those papers with small pages and big print" as Arthur Dent puts it in *Hitchhiker's Guide.* American physicist Murray Gell-Mann is credited with the introduction of the concept of quarks. A small and obscure list, but fun.

Murtagh is an antagonist in the *Eragon* books and protagonist in the *Outlander* series. It's Celtic for protector of the sea.

Mycroft, as everyone knows, is Sherlock Holmes's brother. Traits you're predicting for your child include being a genius but also fat and antisocial. Plus having the spotlight always stolen by a younger brother.

Marvel's Namor the Sub-Mariner is really something of a meanie. If you're naming from the comics, you could at least pick a good guy.

Nan Flanagan is the semi-evil spokesperson for the American Vampire League on *True Blood.* There's the film *Nana,* and Nana Visitor, who played Major Kira on *Star Trek: Deep Space Nine.* The name is a variant on Anne, grace. See Anne.

Nancy is of course linked to *Nancy Drew.* Nancy J. Currie and Nancy Jan Davis were astronauts, while Nancy Kress is a popular fantasy author. *Enchanted* stars Nancy as the practical fiancée, whose dreams finally come true. Not a nasty nomenclature.

Narcissa has a name from Greek myth linked with narcissism. Like many other *Harry Potter* characters, her name reflects her nasty personality.

Nathan "gift from God" stands out for *Firefly* star Nathan Fillion. There's *Star Wars* actress Natalie Portman and fictional characters Nathan Christopher Charles Summers, X-Men's Cable and Nathan Petrelli (*Heroes*). Nathaniel Richards is Young Avengers' Iron Lad. Nathan Rahl is a precognizant hero in *The Sword of Truth.* Nathan West (callsign "King of Hearts") stars in *Space Above and Beyond.* Nathaniel Graison is a were-leopard in the *Anita Blake* books. A gender flip offers Black Widow Natasha Romanov and *Star Trek*'s Tasha Yar.

Nausicaä of the Valley of the Wind is a beloved Manga character with her own series. She's named after Princess Nausica of Greek myth, a lively, independent young lady. Plus, your second child could be No-finda.

Navi is the nickname for the star Gamma Cassiopeiae inveted by astronaut Gus Grissom after his own middle name (Ivan) spelled backwards. Navi (to name in Hebrew) is a title given to Biblical prophets. It's also the name of a character in *The Legend of Zelda.* The Na'vi people in the movie *Avatar* are a referent. There's also Navi Rawat, actress from *Numb3rs* and *The OC.*

Ned see Edward

Neelix…No.

Nemo means no one…a creepy name from either the Jules Verne character or the Pixar fish, cute as you may find the latter.

Neil Armstrong was an astronaut on Gemini 8 and Apollo 11 and the first person to walk on the moon. Niels Bohr made major contributions to understanding atomic structure and quantum theory. And in fiction, Niall Brigant is Sookie Stackhouse's fae ancestor on *True Blood,* with a large role in the books. It's Gaelic for "cloud," "passionate," or "champion," though admittedly it would be best to know for sure. Other illustrious voices in spec fic include *Sandman* and *Coraline* author Neil Gaiman. Neil Patrick Harris plays Dr. Horrible, who has a PhD in horribleness. It's up to you to decide if the value of a higher degree outweighs the questionable choice of major.

The name Nessa is a Greek baby name meaning "Poor, pure, or chaste." Short for Agnes or possible the Loch Ness Monster. Of course, there's also Nessa the Dancer, goddess of Middle earth. Nessarose "Nessa" Thropp is Elphaba's disturbed sister in *Wicked.*

Neville Longbottom is the Gryffindor chump who becomes a hero. Neville has always suggested the chump part, making it a semi-popular British name meaning "new village" in French.

Newt Scamander – Author of *Fantastic Beasts and Where to Find Them,* is probably a worse name than Neville. Other Newts star in *Aliens* and *The Maze Runner*.

Nikki/Nicole gets around as a name: Nikki, from Nicholas, means "victory of the people," while Nike was the Greek goddess of victory. Nicki Clyne plays Crewman Specialist Cally Henderson on new *Battlestar Galactica,* while Nichelle Nichols broke ground as Uhura. Other actors include Nicholas Brendon (Xander), Nicholas Cage (Ghost Rider), and Nicole de Boer (Ezri Dax). Nicole Marie Passonno Stott was an astronaut on STS-128, STS-133. Scientists include Nicholas Culpeper, who fought to make medicine available to everyone, as well as Nicolaus Copernicus, and Nikola Tesla, who's gaining popularity with the Steampunk crowd.

In fiction, Nico di Angelo is a beloved child hero in *Percy Jackson* and Nico is a powerful and clever teen heroine of Marvel's *Runaways.* Nicholas Sayre is a character in Garth Nix's *Abhorsen* series. Nicole Wright is the noble founder of the Vampire Unity Society on *True Blood.* Nikki Wood is a sassy Slayer on *Buffy*. Evil Nicci becomes a heroine in *The Sword of Truth.* Other characters include Nick Fury (*The Avengers*), Nick Fenn (*Being Human* US), Niki Sanders (*Heroes*), Nikolai (*Ender's Shadow* or *Star Trek: The Next Generation*), Nick St. John (*Moonlight*), Nicolas Flamel and Nearly Headless Nick (*Harry Potter*).

Noah Hathaway played the kid in *Battlestar Galactica* and *Neverending Story,* while Noah Bennet is a character in *Heroes.* The name means comfort or long-lived – certainly both good things. #2 in 2015, possibly because of the Biblical film. But too popular can be a problem too. Three happy babies.

Nog is a Ferengi on *DS9* or a holiday beverage. It's unclear which of the two makes this a worse namesake. If used, be comforted that child will be considered a good egg by all.

Norman (meaning Northman) Osborn was the first Green Goblin. Norm Spellman stars in *Avatar*. Norma is the gender flip, of course.

Nuala "white shoulders" is a popular Irish name, the short form of Fionnuala. (The original name belongs to one of the Children of Lir in Irish mythology but is something of a mouthful). Nuala is a princess in *Hellboy II: The Golden Army*, and the selkie character in the film *The Secret of Roan Inish*. She is also a faerie given to Dream at the end of *Season of Mists* in Neil Gaiman's *The Sandman*.

Number Six is a very hot villainess on new *Battlestar Galactica*. Perhaps her lack of a name made her so evil. Confiscating names was equally cruel in *The Prisoner*…

Nymphadora Tonks considers her name just terrible. She goes by Dora or Tonks in *Harry Potter*. Don't condemn your child to be a total tramp, please.

Even the name Oaken, the burly gay proprietor of the eponymous "Wandering Oaken's Trading Post and Sauna," has seen a rise in popularity, going to over five babies in 2013 and 2014 (Wolfers).

Oberon is king of fairyland in Shakespeare's *A Midsummer Night's Dream* and many fantasy novels including *Sandman* comics. Also the liege lord of Amber in *The Chronicles of Amber*. Still weird.

Octavia is a member of Katniss' prep team with pea

green skin and also top scifi author Octavia E. Butler. Octavia on *Princess of Power* is an octopus-like humanoid with four tentacles. This Roman name means born eighth, so you may have many many scifi names to assign.

Odin appears as Thor's father in his comics and in Neil Gaiman's *The Sandman* series. Norse king of the gods, but he did lose an eye in the quest for wisdom. Teach your kid not to do likewise.

Odo, meaning unknown substance in Bajoran, sounds mean. Unless your child is one. Also, Odo Proudfoot attends Bilbo's birthday

Oliver means affectionate. Certainly, fans love Oliver J. Queen – superhero Green Arrow, and Oliver Wood, the Gryffindor Quidditch Keeper and captain. #8 in 2015.

Characters named Olivia (affectionate) appear in *The Stars my Destination, The Selection, My Sister the Vampire,* and *Children of the Red King*.. Of course, there's also Olivia the Pig…

Olympe Maxime – Half-giantess Headmistress of Beauxbatons – has a name that's clearly from Mount Olympus, which towers over Greece. Since the name is meant to mean "devastatingly large" as it applies to the giantess, it's a cruel name for a child.

Oolon Colluphid is the author of several books on religious and other philosophical topics. Colluphid's works include *Where God Went Wrong, Some More of God's Greatest Mistakes, Who Is This God Person Anyway?* in *Hitchhiker's Guide.* It certainly sounds alien…Four sad babies, plus points if he claims to have invented Oolong tea.

Ophelia is Greek for "help" but she doesn't provide

much in *Hamlet*, where she goes mad. The heroine of *Pan's Labyrinth* was named Ofelia in homage. The all-wise Ohlia (Clare Higgens) of the Sisterhood of Karn on *Doctor Who* seems a related name – she's certainly a helper, after all.

Ori is a dwarf in *The Hobbit.* This is Hebrew for light, so less ridiculous than his companions. Aura is a variant.

Orion, a well-known star, is named for the mythic Greek hunter and son of Posideon. In addition, this is the middle name of Sirius Black in *Harry Potter,* the son of Alveric and Lirazel in *The King of Elfland's Daughter* by Lord Dunsany, and the Arquillian jeweler's pet cat in *Men in Black*. It's the name of Artemis's sub-personality from the *Artemis Fowl* books. This was also the name of a capsule mission by NASA and a race of *Star Trek*.

Orko is the small flying nonhuman of *Masters of the Universe*. Sounds like a killer whale.

Orlando, "famous throughout the land" is an Italian variant of Roland. Orlando Bloom, of course, was Legolas and also William Turner from *Pirates.*

Ororo Monroe, Storm of the X-Men, is said to come from Africa. Her name, however, appears to come from Marvel.

Oswald Chesterfield Cobblepot, the Penguin, was abandoned by his parents. I'm sure it's not because he looked like a penguin. Or an Oswald.

Owain was a knight in Arthurian legend. The name means "young warrior; well-born," and is generally spelled Owen. Owen is the 36th most popular boys' name in America, following a steep rise in popularity that began in 1994 (Holeman). There's Uncle Owen from *Star Wars* (better than Beru!), who are the only two people ever to die by Stormtrooper fire. There's Owen Harper on *Torchwood.* These last all end up dead however. Very dead.

Obi-Wan is a great name for a hero of the Clone Wars. Ben might be better for your child. Though the name is fairly popular in the U.K., with 12 American baby boys named Obi in 2014 (Holeman).

Ox from the anime and manga series *Soul Eater* is a powerful but clumsy name. Works with "strong as…" and "dumb as…"

Oy is a "billy-bumbler," which look like a combination of badger, raccoon, and dog, in Stephen King's *Dark Tower* series. Oy.

Oz is both the world of *The Wizard of Oz* and the cool guy on *Buffy*. It's rather oz-scure.

Paige (Latin, "young helper") is one of the main character sisters on *Charmed,* while Paige Elizabeth Guthrie is Husk of the *X-Men.*

Pam is a sassy character on *True Blood.* A namesake, Pamela Melroy, was an astronaut on STS-92, STS-112, STS-120 and Pamela Dean is a fantasy novelist. Dr. Pamela Lillian Isley becomes Poison Ivy. This Greek baby name means "made from honey," appropriate for these seductive female bad girls.

Pan – a chaotic Greek demigod, and Peter Pan's last name (likely related). Panteleimon. "all-merciful" in Greek, is Lyra's daemon spirit in *The Golden Compass.* Since it means "all," you can play with the middle name…or other people can.

Pansy Parkinson is the Slytherin bad girl of Hogwarts and Draco Malfoy's girlfriend. You've been warned.

Parker works as a Peter Parker reference. Also, *Lord of the Rings'* Haldir is played by Craig Parker, and Parker Selfridge stars in *Avatar.* Another Parker is a short-term love interest for Buffy.

Patrick, meaning noble or patrician, is a name held by Patrick Stewart, Professor X and Captain Picard, as well as Patrick Troughton (the Second Doctor). Make it so!

After a gender flip, authors include Patricia A. McKillip and Patricia C Wrede. Tricia Helfer plays Number 6 on new *Battlestar Galactica.* There are a few fictional characters – Tricia McMillan from *Hitchhiker's Guide* and Patty from the anime and manga series *Soul Eater.* Trisana Chandler is a heroine in Tamora Pierce's *Circle of Magic* books. Patsy Stone stars in *Absolutely Fabulous.* And there's Sybill Patricia Trelawney, the Hogwarts Divination professor.

The Biblical Paul ("little") zealously persecuted Christians back when he was called Saul. Famously, he was converted on the road to Damascus and became one of their most fervent supporters. Paul Ballard of *Dollhouse* parallels him spiritually. Another Paul is the protagonist of *Dune.* Pavel Chekhov bears the Russian variant of this name. Colonel Saul Tigh is second in command on new *Battlestar Galactica.* Paul Dierden is a character on *Orphan Black.* 1st Lt. Paul Wang (callsign "Joker") stars in *Space Above and Beyond.* Paul Schafer (later called Pwyll Twiceborn) is a melancholy hero in *The Fionavar Tapestry.* Paula Brooks is Tigress, a comic book character published by DC Comics. She is one of many characters to use the names Tigress and Huntress.

Paul McGann plays the Eighth Doctor on *Doctor Who.* Poul Anderson was a famous author, and Paul Campbell plays Billy Keikeya on new *Battlestar Galactica.* Paul Dirac was an English theoretical physicist and mathematician who founded quantum mechanics and quantum electrodynamics. Finally, Paul Neil Milne Johnstone of Redbridge, Essex, was the writer, according to Adams, of the worst poetry in the universe in *Hitchhiker's Guide.*

Pearl is a sweet name, generally given to fictional mermaids. Also, Pearl Kendrick, an American bacteriologist, helped in co-developing the vaccine for whooping cough.

Peeta, a name invented by *Hunger Games* author Suzanne Collins, may reference pita bread or the Pieta. Peter is the most likely earth variant, if you want him to blend in. Or at least, refrain from self-sacrificing in each book.

Peeves (from *Harry Potter*) means "to irritate" – more of a toddler nickname than an official designation, one hopes.

Peggy see Margaret

Penelope Clearwater is the Ravenclaw prefect and girlfriend of Percy Weasley. She's named for the Greek good wife who spends the entire Odyssey dodging aggressive suitors and waiting for her husband's return. It means bobbin, a domestic sewing tool. Rather housebound compared with Katniss or Xena…

Penny from *The Big Bang Theory* heads the list. Characters named this tend to be children (*Lost in Space, Inspector Gadget, Bolt*) or naive young women (*Hairspray, Doctor Horrible*). "Penny" is a juvenile diminutization of Penelope. Penny Johnson Jerald (actress of Kasidy Yates) and Penny Priddy in *Buckaroo Banzai* join the lineup.

Penryn is the female protagonist in Susan Ee's series *Penryn and the End of Days*. This is a Welsh name meaning legendary. Your child may be this at school…

Percival, a knight in Arthurian legend, has many namesakes. Percival Dumbledore – Father of Albus, is one, and it's one of Albus's middle names. Percy Weasley is another namesake. All fail or have some fatal flaw, like the Arthurian character. One hopes your baby won't develop one himself.

Percy Lavon Julian was one of the first to study the chemical fusion of medicinal plants. Percy Jackson is not named for Percival but Perseus, one of the rarest figures in Greek myth – a success who lived happily ever after.

Peregrin "Pippin" Took was a hero of *Lord of the Rings*…though he starts as a total doofus. This progression is normal for a baby of course.

Peri Brown was a *Doctor Who* companion. Perrin Aybara is a hero in *The Wheel of Time*. Another Perrin married Sarek on *Star Trek*. The name is Greek for "rock."

Peter also means rock. This is of course the name of Spider-Man, Peter Parker. He's Ender's genius yet bullying older brother in *Ender's Game* and the star of *Galaxy Quest*. Pete Tyler is the father of beloved companion Rose Tyler. Two *Doctor Who* actors held this name – Peter Davison (Fifth Doctor) and Peter Capaldi (Twelfth Doctor). Peter Mayhew played Chewbacca. Peter S. Beagle, is author of *The Last Unicorn* and *A Fine and Private Place*. Fantasy offers us Peter Pan, Peter Pevensie of Narnia, and *Harry Potter*'s Peter Pettigrew. An even more villainous one than this is Peter Hayes of *Divergent*. Dr. Peter Venkman is a Ghostbuster. Pete is Carter's love interest on *Stargate*, the best friend on *Smallville,* and characters on *Fringe, Teen Wolf,* and *Heroes.* Other namesakes appear in the folktale Peter and the Wolf and children's film *Pete's Dragon.*

The French version offers us scientists and mathematicians Pierre Curie and Pierre de Fermat. Likewise, Pierre-Simon Laplace was a prominent 19th century mathematical physicist and astronomer. Other areas of the globe give us international X-Men Pietro Django Maximoff (Quicksilver) and Piotr Nikolaievitch Rasputin (Colossus). Petra is a heroine of *Ender's Game* and *Shingeki no Kyojin.* Petyr Baelish is the *Game of Thrones* variant. Peeta is the hero of *The Hunger Games.* Petronella is the first name of Osgood, the fangirl on *Doctor Who.* This last, however, just seems cruel.

Petunia Dursley was Harry Potter's aunt. A nice flower but not a nice lady.

Captain Phasma, female Shocktrooper in *Star Wars VII* is really not a nice lady. Her name isn't so great either.

Phèdre nó Delaunay de Montrève is the heroine in the *Kushiel* series by Jacqueline Carey. She's named for the heroine of Theseus mythology. She warns her readers many times that it's an ill-luck name, which she blames for her problems, however.

Philip is the Disney prince of *Sleeping Beauty.* The name means "lover of horses." Authors include Philip K. Dick and Philip Pullman. Phil Coulson is the leader of *Agents of SHIELD.* Phillip J. Fry is the hero of *Futurama* and Phillip Broyles appears on *Fringe.* For variants, Pippa is a heroine in the YA novel *A Great and Terrible Beauty*, while Pippi Longstocking has delighted generations of children. Her full name is Pippilotta, though Phillippa is more common. In fact, Philippa Hunter is the heroine of one of Madeleine L'Engle's books. Phileas Fogg is the hero of

Around the World in Eighty Days. Philipe Gastone, a thief, stars in *Ladyhawke.*

Phlox sounds like a terminal illness caused by violent diarrhea. In fact, he was the alien on *Star Trek Enterprise,* a show that might be worse than the illness.

Phoebe is another name for Artemis and means bright. One Phoebe appears in *Percy Jackson*, while another is one of the main character sisters on *Charmed.*

Phouchg and Loonquawl received Deep Thought's answer to Life, the Universe, and Everything in *Hitchhiker's Guide.* Phouchg even hurts to say, let alone consider. Their parents were clearly lunkheads.

Famed fantasy-humor author Piers Anthony can certainly distinguish this rare name.

Piper is one of the main character sisters on *Charmed.* Another stars in *Orange is the New Black*, about a yuppie stuck in prison. This last is clearly responsible for the 300% rise in popularity. Presumably the Pied Piper is also a namesake to this trendy American name.

Pit (from the game *Kid Icarus*) suggests having kids is the pits. I wouldn't.

Plutarch Heavensbee of the Hunger Games is named for Roman critic and biographer Mestrius Plutarchus. If you don't live in the Capitol, it seems far too Roman…

Poe Dameron is the handsome hot-shot pilot in *Star Wars VII.* While cooler than cool, he shares a name with the gloomy gothic writer, and works well in playground jokes about the po' kid.

Polly (American, "wished-for child") was a fun sixties *Doctor Who* companion. Polly/Poly (Polyhymnia) O'Keefe is Meg's daughter in the *A Wrinkle in Time* series and a beloved teen hero though you might note that she hates her name from Greek myth. Another child hero is Polly Plummer in the C.S. Lewis books. Polly Perks is a brave cross-dresser in Terry Pratchett's Discworld, who joins the army to find her brother. Polgara the Sorceress and her mother Poledra are heroines of *The Belgariad.* Fun names though highly fantastical and made up.

Pomona Sprout is the rather flighty Hogwarts Herbology professor, named for a Roman harvest goddess. It seems a bit girlier than "apple," anyway.

Poppy Pomfrey is the Hogwarts school nurse. Consider long and hard before naming your child for the flower that produces opium.

Primrose Everdeen is Katniss's heroic little sister in *The Hunger Games.* The English picked primroses for May Day (the beginning of spring) and give them as gifts. The word means the early or youthful rose. As a fairy flower, primroses were used to protect children, while the nickname "Prim" suggests propriety, in contrast with rebellious Katniss. Her name has risen in popularity lately.

Prospero is the hero of *The Tempest.* His name means fortunate, but everyone will see a Shakespearean wizard (for admittedly, double geek points).

Prue is one of the sisters on *Charmed.* It's likely short for the Puritan name Prudence, meaning "practical."

Pteppicymon XXVIII (Teppic) is a hero in Pratchett's Discworld. Sounds like a stew with too many spices.

Puck is a fairy trickster in Shakespeare's *A Midsummer Night's Dream* and many fantasy novels plus *Sandman* comics. Better as a nickname for a mischievous child.

Pythagoras was a mathematical genius. But this must be legalized cruelty to children.

Quark is a nasty little troll on *Star Trek,* with a nasty little mind. Nasty choice.

Quentin in the hapless prince of Dorne in *Game of Thrones,* Latin for five and a common name for a fifth son. Quentin Coldwater stars in Lev Grossman's *The Magicians.* Also Quentin Travers, the unimaginative bureaucrat from *Buffy* and Quentin Lance, father of two Black Canaries on *Arrow.* There's another in *Cube* and one in *Heroes Reborn.*

Questular Rontok is the Vice President of the Galaxy in *Hitchhiker's Guide.* It's likely no worse than Zaphod…

Qui-Gon is only a great namesake if your ancestry is Jedi.

Quinlan Vos was a Jedi Master during the Clone Wars. The name is Gaelic for "shaped as a well." So, with a giant gaping hole in the middle and a swampy smell?

Quintilius Rousse is a hero in the *Kushiel* series by Jacqueline Carey. It means fifth in Latin, hardly a great designator for the kid.

Quirinus Quirrell – Defense Against the Dark Arts professor in Harry's first year, has Lord Voldemort growing out the back of his head. Don't let this happen to your kid.

R2-D2 is too ridiculous and too dorky.

Rachel Anne Grey becomes Phoenix (as the daughter of Jean Grey and Cyclops) (X-Men). American marine biologist, writer and naturalist Rachel Louise Carson is a famous environmentalism and evocative writer. Rachel Roth is Superhero Raven. The name means ewe. Ew.

Radagast, a wizard mentioned as a "cousin" of Gandalf. Now that he's appeared on film covered with bird droppings, he's lost a few cool points. If he ever had any.

Ragnarok from the anime and manga series *Soul Eater* is named for the apocalyptic battle at world's end. Maybe when he hits the terrible twos…

Rakoth Maugrim, the Unraveller, is the dark lord of *The Fionavar Tapestry.* One assumes their parents' naming choices set all these dark lords on this path.

Ramoth is a character in Anne McCaffrey's *The Dragonriders of Pern.* Seems rather teasable.

Ramsay Bolton is the most violent and sadistic person in all of *Game of Thrones.* And that's saying something. He seems to have ruined a nice name, meaning garlic. Perhaps that's part of the torture.

Randolph William "Ralph" Dibny is the Elongated Man. School teacher Ralph Hinkley is another superhero. Of course Ralph is also the idiot child on *The Simpsons* and slang for vomiting. Which the idiot child seems to do often. The name means house-protector or shield-wolf. Rand al'Thor is a hero in *The Wheel of Time.*

Random Frequent Flyer Dent (child of Arthur Dent in *Hitchhiker's Guide*) and Random prince of Amber in *The*

Chronicles of Amber don't really redeem this name. If your pregnancy is a random occurrence, you needn't advertise it.

King Randor is He-Man's father on *Masters of the Universe.* Kind of dinosaur-like.

Ransom is a Cambridge professor kidnapped and taken to Malacandra (Mars) in the C.S. Lewis books. Perhaps his name inspired the kidnappers…

Raphael ("God is healer") is a vampire in *The Mortal Instruments* and also a Ninja Turtle. And a famous artist and an archangel, of course.

Rapunzel is the only Disney and fairytale heroine named after a lettuce. Like Cinderella, it must be considered too cutesy to inflict. Marissa Meyer's fairytale series names her "Cress," short for Crescent Moon, but that seems just as problematic.

Raven Darkholme is Mystique (*X-Men*) and also a dark DC superheroine. Another is a silent woman in *The Mists of Avalon.* There's also Raven Baxter, on *That's So Raven.* Ravens are mysterious, foreboding creatures, with a bonus reference to *Game of Thrones.*

The second Atom was the Silver Age Atom, Ray Palmer. The Ray (real name Raymond C. "Ray" Terrill) is a DC superhero. The name is from rey, king. Dr. Raymond Stantz is a Ghostbuster. Ray Bradbury is one of the fathers of science fiction and Raymond E. Feist writes fantasy. For gender flipping, Reyna is a character in *Percy Jackson* and Raina an antagonist on *Agents of SHIELD.* Another Rayna stars in *After Earth.* Rey of course is the heroine of *Star Wars VII.*

Raziel, the angel of secrets, appears in the game *Soul Reaver,* the books *The Mortal Instruments,* and the *Kushiel* series, among other places. He's a great and terrifying figure, less appropriate for a schoolchild. There's also Fin Raziel of *Willow.*

Razputin was the perfect star for an oddball mental odyssey like *Psychonauts.* As the name of an alleged evil necromancer from Russian history, he's worse than Raziel.

Readis is a character in Anne McCaffrey's *The Dragonriders of Pern.* At least, one assumes, she reads.

Oddly, the name Rebel has surged in popularity, from 10 in 2006 to 55 in 2013 to 46 in 2014 (Holeman). *Hunger Games* or *Star Wars*? Or perhaps eating vegetables?

Reed Richards is Mister Fantastic. It's from the surname meaning "red" or "clearing."

Reepicheep is a hero mouse of Narnia. A wonderful children's book character, though you might aim for a human namesake, or at least a non-rodent.

Rebecca is rare in science-fiction fantasy, though she's a heroine in *Ivanhoe.* Rebecca Buck is Tank Girl. Beka Cooper is a girl-constable heroine of Tamora Pierce's children's books, while Beka Valentine is the heroine of Gene Roddenberry's *Andromeda*

Regan Wyngarde is Lady Mastermind of *X-Men.* Her name comes from the haughty queen of *King Lear,* who, just to warn you, was also a terrible daughter. The name gained popularity after Linda Blair's haunting portrayal of Regan in *The Exorcist*…for some reason. (MooseRoots)

Regina Mills (meaning, appropriately, queen) is the

Evil Queen in *Once Upon a Time.*

Reginald Barclay is the memorable geek of *Star Trek: TNG.* Reginald Cattermole – equally geeky – is an Employee of the Magical Maintenance Department for the Ministry of Magic.

Regulus Arcturus Black is Sirius Black's mildly traitorous brother, named by a family who thought they all needed to be objects on a star chart. Beware this naming pattern if this is the result.

Remus Lupin is a *Harry Potter* hero. He's named for a Roman ancestor raised by a wolf. Since both characters get killed and have a wolfy side, there may be better choices out there.

Remy "oarsman" is from the French saint of this name. This is the name of X-Men hero, Gambit, Remy LaBeau. There's also a Remy in *Ratatouille.*

Rene/Renee ("reborn" in French) lends its name to a villain of *True Blood.* She's the mother in *Twilight,* while Renee Palmer is the action heroine of *Earth: Final Conflict.* René Auberjonois plays Odo on *Deep Space Nine.* René Descartes was a famed philosopher.

CT-7567, nicknamed Rex, was a clone trooper captain during the Clone Wars. Rex is also a popular name for a dog. DO keep that in mind.

The name Rey, "king," is steadily rising among American boys. Over 240 were born in 2014, up from just 46 in 1980 (Holeman). This name belongs to the (admittedly female) tough survivor from the deserts of Jakku in *The Force Awakens.*

Rhea was the Greek mother goddess, who gave birth to Zeus. Rhea Silvia is a character in *Percy Jackson,* embodying the goddess's Roman counterpart. Decrepit old witch Rhea Dubativo and her 6 legged mutant cat appear in in Stephen King's *Dark Tower* series. Rhea Seddon, M.D., was an astronaut on STS-51-D, STS-40, STS-58. Rhea Jones is also the name of a female comic book superhero created by Paul Kupperberg and owned by DC Comics. She at times went by the alias Lodestone

Rhys (the benevolent husband of *Torchwood*) has a Welsh name that means rashness (so be on your guard if you go this route). For a possible flip, Resa is the heroine's mother in *Inkheart.*

Richard Castle solves crimes while popping into pop culture worlds. He has many namesakes, all meaning "strong ruler." Kings include Richard the Lionheart and Richard III. Richard Cypher is the star of Terry Goodkind's giant epic series and the *Sword of Truth* television show. Richard is a main character in the Anita Blake books and there's small sidekick Richard John "Dick" Grayson.. There's Author Rick Riordan and actor Richard Dean Anderson from *Stargate.* Richard Hatch plays the original Apollo and Tom Zarek on *Battlestar Galactica.*

Richard "Dick" Scobee was an astronaut on STS-41-C. He died on the Challenger. Richard F. Gordon, Jr. was an astronaut on Gemini 11 and Apollo 12. Gordon was selected to command the Apollo 18 lunar landing, which was later cancelled.

Riley ("valiant") is a hero and boyfriend on *Buffy.* It's a popular surname, growing as a first name for both genders. Namesakes include Riley Poole in the *National Treasure* movies and Riley Biers, a character in the *Twilight Saga.*

Rilian is the son of Caspian of Narnia. If it was a real name, it would probably mean laughter. And besides, it's not.

Rincewind is the inept and cowardly hero of Discworld. There are more heroic namesakes there with less awkward names.

Rinya, priestess of Dune, may have a name similar to Reina, queen.

River Song and River Tam, each superheroines, add sparkle to this bubbly nature name. "The symbolism of rivers and running water is simultaneously that of 'universal potentiality' and that of 'the fluidity of forms' of fertility, death, and renewal" (Chevalier and Gheerbrant 808).

Ro Laren is a hero on *Star Trek*, though this name could be short for nearly anything in English.

Roald Dahl is the beloved author of many many children's books, though another unusual choice.

Robert, "bright fame," has many namesakes. The Almighty Bob is a deity worshipped by the people of Lamuella in *Hitchhiker's Guide*. Robert Baratheon and Robb Stark hail from *Game of Thrones*. Rupert Giles, Robin Wood, and Robert Flutie all appear in *Buffy*. Lisa Milbrand wrote in *Parents Magazine* that "neither Buffy's guiding force, Watcher Rupert Giles, nor Rupert Grint, the actor who played Ron Weasley in the *Harry Potter* series, was able to bring this name into prominence in the U.S. (It is still pretty popular in the UK, though)." *Enchanted* stars Giselle, who falls for her American Robert. Robert "Hob" Gadling is a human granted immortality in Neil Gaiman's

The Sandman. There's "Bobby" Drake, the X-Man Iceman, and Bobby Singer (*Supernatural*). Robur is a Jules Verne creation, from the novels *Robur the Conqueror* and *Master of the World. Forbidden Planet* offers Robby the Robot.

There are too many authors to count, including Robert A. Heinlein, early game designer Roberta Williams, Robert Asprin, Robert E. Howard, creator of *Conan the Barbarian* and *Tarzan*, and Robert Jordan, author of *The Wheel of Time.* Robert Beltran, Robert Picardo, and Robert Duncan McNeill all starred on *Star Trek: Voyager.* Robert Pattinson was on *Twilight.*

There's a long list of scientists here: Robert Bosch, Robert Boyle, Robert Brown, Robert Bunsen, Robert Goddard, Robert Hooke, Robert Koch, and J. Robert Oppenheimer, also known as "the father of the atomic bomb." Roberta Bondar, M.D. was a Canadian astronaut on STS-42.

Holy naming guides, Batman! "Robin" comes from Robert, "bright fame," though it also suggests the bird. Robin Hood is the obvious namesake, though there's also Christopher Robin and Robin the Boy Wonder. The fairy trickster Robin or Puck appears in many fantasy stories. Robin Williams has played many sf and f roles himself. The male *Buffy* fighter and principal Robin Wood is named for film critic Robin Wood, whom producer Joss Whedon admires. Robin Lefler, the spunky love interest for Wesley Crusher from *Star Trek* is another namesake. For a variant, Robinton is a character in Anne McCaffrey's *The Dragonriders of Pern.*

Rocky DeSantos is a Mighty Morphin Power Ranger. He shares his name with Stalone's Rocky, but also the *Rocky Horror Picture Show* and the flying squirrel.

Roderick Burgess (1863–1947) was the Lord Magus of The Order of the Ancient Mysteries in *The Sandman.*

Rodolphus Lestrange was a Death Eater, husband of Bellatrix Lestrange. Rodrigo López de Segura (1540-1580) authored the definitive book on chess. Rod Sterling was the genius behind *The Twilight Zone.* Roderick means "famous ruler" in German. Also, Rodney McKay is the arrogant doofus scientist of *Stargate: Atlantis.*

Roger "famous warrior" has many namesakes. On *Angel,* there are parents to heroes Roger Burkle and Roger Wyndam-Pryce. Roger Chaffee was an astronaut who died in the Apollo 1 fire. Roger Zelazny wrote *The Chronicles of Amber.* Characters include Roger, the alien from *American Dad*, Pongo's owner in *101 Dalmatians,* and a bad boy in *Lord of the Flies.* There's also Duke Roger of Conte, main antagonist in the *Song of the Lioness* quartet. Roger Parslow is a hero of the *Golden Compass* series. And another – Sgt Roger Murtaugh – is too old for this…stuff.

Roland, Germanic for famous land, lends its name to *Sweetheart Roland* and *The Song of Roland* from fantasy's great predecessors. Another stars in Stephen King's *Dark Tower* series. Rolan is a magical horse in Mercedes Lackey's *Valdemar* books. Rolande de la Courcel is a hero in the *Kushiel* series by Jacqueline Carey. Rolanda Hooch is the Hogwarts flying instructor.

Rom (*Deep Space Nine*) and Romana (*Doctor Who* companion) are a lovely pair of characters from science fiction. Another appears in Hasbro licensed Marvel Comic *SpaceKnight.* Both names sound like they *could* be earth names, but you could just go with a more traditional American one from nearby on this list.

Romilda Vane is the Hogwarts Student with a crush on Harry. He doesn't like her, possibly because of her clunky name.

Ron Weasley is the obvious association for Ronald (though Ronald McDonald will last forever in children's minds). The name is Celtic for counselor. There are other spec fic associations, as Ronald D. Moore was showrunner for *Battlestar Galactica, Star Trek: DS9,* and *Outlander,* and Ron Glass plays Shepherd Book on *Firefly.* Ronald Rust is a blustering general in Terry Pratchett's Discworld and Ronald Sandoval is a complex antihero in *Earth: Final Conflict.* Astronaut Ronald McNair died on the Challenger.

Ronan is Irish for little seal, suggesting your child may be a selkie. Presumably a cute one. Ronan Nolan, Jr is a wizard in *A Wizard Abroad*, while Ronon Dex is the warrior of *Stargate: Atlantis.*

Roosta is a hitchhiker and researcher for the Guide in *Hitchhiker's Guide*, who really knows where his towel is. Sounds kind of like the barnyard bird.

The most famous Rory is probably the beloved *Doctor Who* companion. This is also the name of Gale's little brother in *The Hunger Games.* Roran Garrowsson is Eragon's cousin in the *Inheritance Cycle.* Gaelic for "red king," it's the name of several medieval Irish kings.

Rose Tyler is not just a *Doctor Who* companion, but the one who arguably revived the series. The name references the flower, of course. Disney's Sleeping Beauty has this name, as do many fairytale princesses like Snow-White & Rose-Red. In this tradition, Rose Walker is a fictional character from the Neil Gaiman's *Sandman* series. Rose Psychic is a DC Comics heroine working with Doctor Occult.

Real life heroine Rosalind Franklin discovered A and B forms of DNA while Rosalind Chao plays *Star Trek*'s Keiko. Rosalind Solomon is an agent of S.H.I.E.L.D.

Rosie becomes Sam's wife in *Lord of the Rings* (finally – a name from Tolkien you can get away with!). Rose McGowan played one of the main character sisters on *Charmed.* There's a Rose in the *Ender's Game* series, and Hermione and Ron name their daughter this. There's Rose Dawson (*Titanic*), Rosalie Cullen (*Twilight*), Rose-Marie (*The Vampire Diaries*), Rose Ashby (*The Chemical Gardens Trilogy*), and Rose Hathaway (*The Vampire Academy*).

For variants, Rosanna is Dustfinger's child in *Inkheart,* and Rosella, a heroine of the *King's Quest* computer games (and one of the first active heroines of any computer game). Rosethorn, with plant magic, is a magical teacher at Winding Circle (*Circle of Magic*). Rosie Palm is a practical lady of negotiable virtue in Terry Pratchett's Discworld. Madam Rosmerta runs the Three Broomsticks in Harry Potter's neighboring village. And don't forget Primrose Everdeen from *The Hunger Games.*

Rowena of British legend, wife to High King Vortigern is the namesake of Ivanhoe's ladylove. Both lend their names to Rowena Ravenclaw, one of the founders of Hogwarts. It's pretty, but it's pretty Celtic, likely Germanic for fame and joy. Rowley might be considered the genderflip here – Rowley Eardwulf is a merchant in *The Elder Scrolls.*

Roxanne is a romantic name, held by Alexander the Great's wife and the heroine of *Cyrano de Bergerac.* It means dawn in Persian. Roxane is also Dustfinger's wife in *Inkheart,* while Roxanne de Mereliot is a heroine in the *Kushiel* series by Jacqueline Carey. Roxanne is also a *Pokémon* character. Roxanne Dawson stars in *Star Trek: Voyager* and *Daredevil.*

Roy Mustang hails from anime. In fact, Roy means king. True, Roy Neary (Richard Dreyfuss) stars in *Close Encounters of the Third Kind*…but you'd better watch out for mashed potato sculptures.

Rubeus Hagrid holds a made-up J.K. Rowling name, meaning red. Suitable for a Celtic god or Viking more than your kid.

Rue is a small yellow flower that grows in the meadow and also Katniss's beloved sidekick in *The Hunger Games* who dies tragically young. Her name has risen in popularity lately. The rue is a small, hardy, evergreen plant; like the Katniss, that flourishes in a world of few nutrients. Its bitter taste created the English verb "rue," to wish that something had never happened. The rue plant was called Herb-of-Grace, with an older Roman name *Ruta* from the Greek *reuo* (to set free), because this herb cures some diseases and poisons. A sweet girl, but names with dictionary meanings (especially negative ones) always suggest extra thought.

Related to Rebeus is Rufus, also meaning red. Rufus Drumknott is Vetinari's secretary in Terry Pratchett's Discworld. Another appears in *The Rescuers,* and one as the tough Minister of Magic in *Harry Potter.* Old-fashioned and British, but if he's got really red hair and you really need to inform everyone of that…

Rullgardina is the Swedish equivalent of "Windowshade" and Pippi Longstocking's middle name. Seems funnier in Swedish (doesn't everything?). Swedish or English, it'll certainly make an impression…

Russell (another name meaning Red, this one French) is Fenchurch's burly, blonde-moustached, blow-dried brother in *Hitchhiker's Guide.* There's another in *Up.* Russell Edgington is the evil vampire king of Mississippi on *True Blood.* Russell L. "Rusty" Schweickart was an astronaut on Apollo 9. And of course, Russell T Davies was the one to revive *Doctor Who.*

Ruth is a character in Anne McCaffrey's *The Dragonriders of Pern,* while Ruth Bat-Seraph is X-Man Sabra. This Hebrew Biblical name means companion; friend; vision of beauty.

Lord Ruthven was one of the original literary vampires. Ruthven is also a vampiric rabbit often seen in the background in Neil Gaiman's *The Sandman.*

Ryan, Celtic for "little king," lends his name to the Atom, Ryan Choi. Seems that's all this popular name has got.

Saavik is a friend of Spock, his wife in the books. Don't make me laaugh.

Sabrina the teenage witch is a delightful heroine. "Sabrina was everyone's favorite teenage witch in the 1990s, and the name did become slightly more popular in the U.S. after 1996. What affected the name most significantly was the 1954 film *Sabrina* starring Audrey Hepburn" (MooseRoots). Her name is Latin for the Isle of Cyprus, Aphrodite's birthplace. Watch for young magical abilities.

Sabriel is the protagonist in Garth Nix's *Abhorsen* series. Her name might mean "the rest of God." Made up by the author, but certainly plausible as an angel name.

Sacharissa Cripslock is a heroine in Terry Pratchett's Discworld. Talk about sticky sweet!

Sadie Kane stars in *The Kane Chronicles* by Rick Riordan. It means princess and certainly highlights another young female protagonist. For a true geek reference, Sadie Peterson Delaney was the American librarian who pioneered bibliotherapy. Yes, really.

Saffron Monsoon stars in *Absolutely Fabulous*. Another Saffron is the delightful bad girl of *Firefly* though that's almost certainly not her real name. Spicy and rather flower-child-like.

Salazar Slytherin, semi-evil co-founder of Hogwarts, has a name that was originally a Spanish Basque surname meaning "old hall." Ironically, Hogwarts is indeed that. If you name the kid this, he may turn to evil, however. Or at least display a snake fixation.

Sally Ride was the first American woman in space. Other Sallys appear in *The Nightmare Before Christmas* and *Being Human* (US). There's also a Salacia in Discworld. The name was originally short for Sarah, "princess," but now is used independently.

Sam is said to mean sun child; bright sun, while Samuel/Samwell means "God has heard." In the Bible, he was a great prophet. Obviously, everyman Sam in *Lord of the Rings* and his namesake in *Game of Thrones* would actually be an appropriate homage in these modern times without the strangeness of Hodor or Gandalf. Sam Merlotte is a romantic lead on *True Blood*. Scientist Sam Beckett stars in *Quantum Leap*. "Samantha is the sweet, spunky witch from the 1960s TV show *Bewitched*. The name shot to popularity in 1965, one year after the show aired, and has been in the top-200 in the U.S. ever since" (MooseRoots). Samantha Carter is beloved as the tough soldier-scientist of *Stargate*, while Sam Winchester (*Supernatural*) is beloved as a demon fighter and hottie. Samuel T. Anders is a sports star and love interest on new *Battlestar Galactica*. Samuel Zachary Guthrie is Cannonball

(*X-Men*). Sam Parkhill is a protagonist in Bradbury's *Martian Chronicles.*

Actor Sam Worthington stars in *Avatar.* Finally, Samuel Clemmens deserves some credit as Mark Twain for writing several fantasy adventures. For odd variants, Sameth is the son and younger child of Sabriel in Garth Nix's *Abhorsen* series and Samus Aran of the game Metroid, shockingly revealed himself to be a woman in disguise.

"Before you die … you see the ring." The creepy film *The Ring* starred the ghost Samara (Hebrew for "Protected by God"). "In 2003 and 2004, there were over 400 more Samaras born than usual, but the name has since decreased in popularity" (MooseRoots).

Sandra Magnus was an astronaut on several missions while Sandra Bennet stars in *Heroes.* Sandrilene fa Toren (Sandry) is a heroine in Tamora Pierce's *Circle of Magic* books, but even the author is likely tired of writing all those letters. Sandor Clegane seems a logical gender flip from *Game of Thrones*…it could be a name, though it has more than a touch of medieval or perhaps alien – Sandor smash! Sandor will destroy you! Ser Sandor Clegane had four real-life babies named for him recently (Poladian).

Sansa Stark has a name that's a variant on sun. She seems the pushover princess of *Game of Thrones,* but she learns to manipulate and survive. To say nothing of the hairstyles… "Arya saw a bump in popularity, with 244 babies, while her older sister Sansa had six babies named after her" (Poladian). It seems she can't escape the comparison.

Saphira Bjartskular is Eragon's beloved dragon in the *Inheritance Cycle.* The name can be Hebrew for story or book as well as sapphire. Mystical but you can likely get away with it.

Sarah, Hebrew for princess, has a few wonderful namesakes. There's Sarah Connor from everything *Terminator,* Sara Kingdom (early *Doctor Who* companion), Sarah Jane Smith (possibly the most beloved *Doctor Who* companion), Sarah from *Labyrinth*, Sarah, the star of *Orphan Black.* Real people include Australian epic fantasy author Sara Douglass or Buffy actress Sarah Michelle Gellar. Sarah Rushman is Marrow of the X-Men, while Sarah Walker stars on *Chuck.* Lots of extra points for all these references. See Sally, Sadie.

Sarek is Spock's father. With a classic Vulcan name. Are you ethnically Vulcan?

Saruman is the evil wizard of *Lord of the Rings.*

Satan, an alternate name for the devil, gives his name to Satan SaDiablo (*Dark Jewels Trilogy*) and Sha'tan (*Wheel of Time*). Don't pass it to your kid.

Saul see Paul

Sauron's name sounds like a primeval lizard. And he is in fact prime evil. His name reflects it.

Savage Opres, brother of Darth Maul, has a truly evil name, without any attempt to hide it. You wouldn't…

Scabior – The Snatcher who captures Harry Potter, Ron Weasley and Hermione Granger in Deathly Hallows. Possibly the worst name ever, even if he's covered in scabs.

Scarlet is not just from *Gone with the Wind* anymore. There's Marissa Meyer's fairytale heroine (Red Riding

Hood) and Terry Goodkind's dragon heroine. The first has questionable morals, however.

Schmendrick is a bumbling magician hero in *The Last Unicorn.* The word, of course, is an insult. And a bear to spell.

Scorpius: From *Farscape* or *Harry Potter,* it seems like an ill-omened, serpentine name.

Scott, meaning Scottish or wanderer, is headed by Scott Summers, Cyclops of the X-Men. There's also Scott Bakula (from *Star Trek: Enterprise* and *Quantum Leap*) and Scott of *Teen Wolf.* Scott Carpenter was an astronaut on Mercury 7 and Scott Westerfeld is a popular young adult author.

Seamus Finnigan is an Irish Gryffindor student and Harry's friend. Seamus Harper is a hero on Gene Roddenberry's *Andromeda.* It's the Gaelic variant on James, he who supplants. See James

Sean Cassidy is Banshee of the X-Men. There are several excellent actors, including Sean Connery (James Bond, King Arthur, and many other roles), Sean Maher (Simon Tam), Sean Astin (Sam Gamgee), and Sean Bean (*Game of Thrones, Lord of the Rings).* The name is the Irish John, "God is gracious." See John

Sebastian ("revered") is a villain in *The Mortal Instruments* and *X-Men* and a big crab in *The Little Mermaid.* Literally. Sebastian Michaelis is a demon in anime. Anne Bishop has an Incubus wizard named Sebastian as hero. Finally, Bastian is the hero of *The Neverending Story.* A bit old fashioned and occult, but perhaps he'll become a hero.

Selena ("moon") is Aquagirl as well as Eragon's

mother in the *Inheritance Cycle*. Another Selina is Catwoman. Selenay is a heroine queen in Mercedes Lackey's Valdemar books. Silena Beauregard is a love interest in *Percy Jackson*. There's a Selene in *Underworld*. All intriguing and exotic.

Seneca was a Roman Stoic philosopher, humorist and playwrite. He was ordered to commit suicide when implicated in another's crime, thus providing a namesake for Seneca Crane, the head Gamemaker on *The Hunger Games*. At least your child will grow an impressively twisty beard…

Septima Vector is Arithmancy professor at Hogwarts. Perhaps she has six siblings? Septimus from *Stardust* actually does.

Lord Sepulchrave is the perished patriarch of *Gormenghast*. His name is appropriate for a dead character or possibly a funeral director.

Serenity is called the tenth character of *Firefly*. It's a peaceful name, but there are more conventional options. This also works as an homage to the Serenity prayer, though this is often said at AA meetings.

Scientist Seth Brundle becomes the Fly, while Seth Green starred on *Buffy* and other shows and went on to produce *Robot Chicken*. The Biblical name is Hebrew for "Anointed."

Seven of Nine…you wouldn't…would you? Even if you had nine kids and you wanted an amoral space babe in tight clothes, you'd give her a real name, right? Seven's is actually Annika, if you want to know.

Severio Stregazza is a benevolent though fiery

character in Jacqueline Carey's *Kushiel* series. Severus Snape is the complex Head of Slytherin House in *Harry Potter,* lusted after by much of fandom. These mean "severe," of course. Servalan of *Blake's 7* is related. Bringing this back to real life, there's also Severo Ochoa, Nobel prize Laureate who synthesized RNA.

Shae is a traitor/prostitute in *Game of Thrones.* Who dies violently. Shame on you for considering it.

Shannon is Irish for "wise river." Shannon Lucid was an astronaut on several missions, as was Shannon Walker. Shannen Doherty played one of the main character sisters on *Charmed.* Capt. Shane Vansen (callsign "Ace of Diamonds," later "Queen of Diamonds") stars in *Space Above and Beyond.* Plus Shane was that gunslinger from the classic novel.

Sharon is a poignant Cylon on new *Battlestar Galactica.* It means "plains" in Hebrew.

Sharra is a character in Anne McCaffrey's *The Dragonriders of Pern.* Hebrew for singer.

She-Ra is the heroine of *Princess of Power.* Better go with her secret identity, Adora. Or get her a very tiny plastic sword.

Shea Ohmsford is the protagonist of *The Sword of Shannara.* It's Irish for "majestic," but like the novels, somewhat out of fashion.

Sheldon from *The Big Bang Theory* has a name that means "valley with steep sides" in Old English. It was chosen to be on the geeky side. "Bazinga!"

Sheri S. Tepper is a top feminist science fiction author.

The name is French for darling, also related to Sharon.

Sherlock will get lots of teasing, though possibly a lucrative independent detective business or various unsavory habits.

Shiara (little and womanly) is a sparking heroine in Patricia C. Wrede's *Enchanted Forest Chronicles*. Another is an ancestress in *Game of Thrones* and a truly captivating woman. Shiera Sanders Hall is DC's Hawkgirl.

Shirl Ravenlock is basically the only woman in *The Sword of Shannara,* but that doesn't get her a lot of points.

Sid is from Sidney, Wide Island. Sid appears in Ice Age and in the anime and manga series *Soul Eater*. Cyd Sherman is heroine Codex on *The Guild*. "Sidney was already becoming a popular name in the U.S. when the film *Scream* debuted in 1996. The popularity of the film and the following sequels helped put the name Sidney in the top 300 from 1997 to 2001" (MooseRoots). Sidonie de la Courcel is the hero-princess in the *Kushiel* series by Jacqueline Carey.

Sidious – a very insidious and evil name given to the empreor in *Star Wars*. Plus, evil wrinkles.

Sigmund Freud was a groundbreaking psychologist, while mythic Sigmund was a great warrior from Norse myth, father of Siegfried the dragon slayer. The name means "victorious protector," but we've entered operatic German territory.

American actress Sigourney Weaver adopted the name Sigourney in 1963 after a minor character in *The Great Gatsby,* "Mrs. Sigourney Howard." It's an American last name. It's rather unique thanks to its origin, but would allow you to salute the actress from *Alien, Avatar, Ghostbusters,* and a host of other films.

In the Bible, Simon ("listen") was the name of two apostles. Scifi heroes include Simon Belmont (the game *Castlevania*), Simon Drew, child hero of *The Dark is Rising*, Simon Lewis is a hero in *The Mortal Instruments,* as Simon Tam in on *Firefly*. Simon Baz is a fictional comic book superhero appearing in books published by DC Comics, usually in those starring the Green Lantern Corps, Simon Kemplar is Bladezz on *The Guild.* Imagine how much fun it'll be sharing all these with your son. And he'll be a good listener, too.

Sirius Black, Harry Potter's godfather, is named for the dog star. It's siriusly strange for a name.

Skeeve, a young journeyman magician from *Myth Adventures,* and Skif, a young thief hero in Mercedes Lackey's *Valdemar* books, both betray their shifty origins with shifty and skeevy names.

Skeletor is the villain of *Masters of the Universe.* Like other supervillains, he's *very* hokey. Extra points for a younger brother named MummRa.

Sky/Skye is a young superheroine in *Agents of SHIELD* and *The Sarah Jane Adventures.* A lovely, heavenly name.

Slartibartfast in *Hitchhiker's Guide* was certainly teased in school. There's no question.

"Hey you guys!" Sloth of *The Goonies* has a terrible name. Even if your baby is really lazy.

Smaug is the last of the great dragons. Then an exdragon. Also a villain. And a bad naming option. Never name your child after an on the-nose social metaphor.

Supreme Leader Snoke, supervillain played by Andy Serkis in *Star Wars VII,* has a silly supervillain name. Might as well go for Snookie.

Sookie is a variation of Sukey, a pet form of Susanna, "lily." Sookie Stackhouse is the heroine of *True Blood.* But are the fairy powers worth the vampires?

Sorsha, heroine of *Willow,* shares her name with Juliet Marillier's lovely heroine Sorcha. It's Gaelic for brightness.

Sophia means wisdom, seen in *Walking Dead* and *Yu-Gi-Oh!* There's also a Sophie in Roald Dahl's *The BFG* and Dan Brown's *DaVinci Code.* Craig and Sophie are sweet ordinary folk on *Doctor Who.* #1 in 2014 and #3 in 2015.

Sparta, the ancient city of Greece, is certainly tempting. It *sounds* like a girl's name. And imagine your joy traveling the land explaining, "THIS IS Sparta!" Maybe not. Of course, when obligated to eat a subpar holiday meal at a relative's house, she would be permitted to say "Tonight, we dine in HELL!!"

Spike Spiegel is a cooler than cool hero from *Cowboy Bebop,* arguably an early steampunk series. Of course, Spike, a fairy in Holly Black's *Fairie Court,* shares a name with the bad-boy vampire of *Buffy.* Plus, prearmed.

Spock was a child psychologist as well as the beloved Trek alien. Your kid may emulate the latter, but will need the former…

Squatterbloat was a demon of Hell and guardian of the Gates of Hell in Neil Gaiman's *The Sandman.* He has the distinction of having one of the worst names in the universe.

Sssqueeze is a *Masters of the Universe* villain. Extra s's and all. Ssso bad.

Stacy see Anastasia

Stanley ("from the rocky clearing") gives us Marvel creator Stan Lee and also Stan Shunpike, conductor of the Knight Bus. Literally, the name rocks There's ultra-macho Stan on *American Dad* and Stan of *South Park*.. A possibly related name is Stannis Baratheon, though you risk your child having truly dysfunctional family relationships.

Star can certainly be an homage to *Star Trek, Star Wars,* and even *Stargate* (as well as those lights in the sky). There's also *Stargirl,* the novel by Jerry Spinelli, and Star Butterfly, the Princess from Disney's *Star vs. the Forces of Evil.* Starfire in DC's *Teen Titans* is a rather superhero-y variant.

Starbuck is a hotshot pilot on new *Battlestar Galactica.* In the new version, her real name is Kara. The latter may help the kid avoid a coffee fixation.

Stark is the surname of Avengers hero Ironman aka Tony Stark and the heroes of *Game of Thrones.* Sounds a bit...stark though. And they're all ill-fated families.

Stephen/Steven is multifaceted as expected. Between Steve Rogers and Stephen Hawking, there's plenty of geek cred. Creators include Stephen Moffatt, Stephen King, Stephenie Meyer, and Steven Spielberg. Steve Austin is the Six Million Dollar Man, Steven Taylor is a *Doctor Who* companion, and Stephen Franklin is the doctor on *Babylon 5*. Stephanie Brown is Batgirl (one of them). Dr. Stephen

Strange is Marvel's magician. There's Stevie Atkins (*Being Human US*). Stefen is a hero in Mercedes Lackey's Valdemar books and a hot vampire on *The Vampire Diaries.*

In the real world, Steven Chu is known for his work on trapping atoms using laser light, which won him the Nobel Prize in Physics. Stephanie Wilson was an astronaut on STS-121, STS-120, STS-131, while Stephanie Kwolek was an organic chemist, best known for inventing Kevlar in 1965.

Stinkor, Evil Master of Odor, is a *Masters of the Universe* villain. Really. While you may feel inspired by the diaper smell, keep the nickname temporary.

Strax is a dumpy potato-shaped alien with no neck. And mammary glands. Is that what you want?

Stuart means steward, keeper of the animal enclosure, and became a name of kings. There's actor Patrick Stewart. Also, Stuart Roosa was an astronaut on Apollo 14, while Stuart from *The Big Bang Theory* is a struggling comic book store owner. Stewy on *Family Guy* is probably a Stewart. Thus they run the entire spectrum of scifi fame and fortune.

Summer Glau stars in *Firefly* and *The Sarah Connor Chronicles.* A warm name.

Sunny Baudelaire is a main character of Lemony Snicket's *A Series of Unfortunate Events.* A bright, breezy, happy name.

Surreal SaDiablo is an assassin heroine in *The Black Jewels Trilogy*. Kinda surreal.

Susan is Death's granddaughter in Discworld, given a deliberately ordinary name or circumvent her destiny, which doesn't work. The name means lily. Susan/Suzanne is very popular on *Babylon 5* with Susan Ivanova and many other characters carrying it. There's Susan Pevensie of Narnia and Suzanna Waite (*Being Human* US). Susan Bones the Hufflepuff student and Susan Foreman, the first *Doctor Who* companion. Susannah Dean stars in Stephen King's *Dark Tower* series, as does Susan Delgado.

Suzanne Collins is the beloved author of *The Hunger Games* and Susan Cooper, of *The Dark Is Rising*. Susan Helms and Susan Still Kilrain were astronauts. Sue Dibny is a superhero, like Sue Storm. James "Jim" Barr and Susan Kent-Barr were Golden Age Bulletman and Bulletgirl. There's a giant woman called this in *Monsters vs Aliens* and another (normal-sized one) in *I, Robot*. Suzanne Chan is Sway of the X-Men. Superheroism seems guaranteed.

Sibyl means prophetess in Greek. Fittingly, Sybill Patricia Trelawney is the Hogwarts Divination professor. Sybil Mira has mind magic in Marissa Meyer's fairytale series, though she's a villainess.

Sycorax is Caliban's evil mother in *The Tempest*. This name was used for a race of *Doctor Who* villains. That's two sad babies already, plus more for sounding like a dinosaur.

Sylar is Gabriel Gray's fake name as he is the primary antihero in the NBC drama *Heroes* and targets other superhumans in order to steal their powers. Perhaps he's related to *Star Trek* Vulcan Selar, or has a brother Kevlar.

Sylvester McCoy (Seventh Doctor) has a name that means woodlands. Sylvester Stallone and Sylvester the cat share the name.

Tabitha Smith is Boom-Boom of the *X-Men*. Means "gazelle" in Aramaic. In the New Testament, Tabitha was a woman restored to life by Saint Peter. Another hails from *Bewitched.*

Tahmoh Penikett acts in *Man of Steel, Dollhouse,* and new *Battlestar Galactica.* The actor chose this name for himself from a word from the Canadian Tanana tribe. But he hasn't revealed its meaning.

Talia is a telepath heroine on *Babylon 5,* a teen heroine in Mercedes Lackey's Valdemar books, and the mother of Batman's son Damien. Another Talia was a part of the Nightsisters clan during the *Star Wars* Clone Wars. Talia is a Hebrew name meaning "dew from God." Several Sleeping Beauties go by this name. Variants include Talisa Stark from *Game of Thrones*, Talo from the *Ender's Game* series, and Talan from *The Elder Scrolls.* Thalia, meanwhile, is a Greek muse and one of the Graces. Since it can be short for Natalia, see Nathan for more homages.

Tamara is from the Biblical Tamar, "date palm" (and a rather shocking story of heroic incest). Tamara E. Jernigan was an astronaut on STS-40, STS-52, STS-67, STS-80, STS-96. Tammy Reynolds is a witch is a main character in the *Anita Blake* books. With a variant spelling, Tamora Pierce is a beloved children's fantasy author. Tarma is a heroine in Mercedes Lackey's Valdemar books.

Tananda, a.k.a. Tanda, is a professional assassin from *Myth Adventures.* She's also a Trollop. This is her species, not a value judgment, but you've been warned.

Tandy Bowen is Dagger from the Marvel universe. Oddly, the name is short for Andrew, or possibly Andrea.

Tanith, Semitic for "serpent lady," was the name of the Phoenician goddess of love, fertility, the moon and the stars. Also beloved fantasy author Tanith Lee.

Tārā is the name of a set of bodhisattvas, or Buddhist deities, of mercy and compassion. Tara Thornton is a sassy character on *True Blood*, while Tara Maclay is a gentle witch on *Buffy*. The name means earth, suggesting comfort and protective feminine magic.

Taran Wanderer is Assistant Pig-Keeper and hero of *The Chronicles of Prydain.* His name comes from the Welsh *Mabinogion*, as a thunder-god who also inspired the name of Taran mac Ainftech, a Pictish king from the 7th century.

"One does not judge the gazelle by the lions that attack it." But one definitely prejudges a kid named Tarzan.

Tate is a *Pokémon* character and appears in *American Horror Story*. It means cheerful.

Taylor Lautner plays Jacob Black in *Twilight* and another appears in *Planet of the Apes.* The unisex name in fact means tailor, unsurprisingly. Tayla is a butt-kicking warrior on *Stargate: Atlantis.*

Ted is short for Theodore (gift of God). Namesakes include Ted Tonks, grandfather of Teddy Remus Lupin in *Harry Potter.* Ted King plays Prue's first love Andy Trudeau on *Charmed.* Thaddeus Thawne aka Inertia is a villain from The Flash, but this seems a stuffy variant. See Theodore

Teela is the fighter heroine of *Masters of the Universe.* It could be a name, one supposes.

Tegan (Welsh for beautiful) was a *Doctor Who* companion. An unusual choice that will get her science fiction points if anyone knows the reference.

Telemain a pompous magician in Patricia C. Wrede's *Enchanted Forest Chronicles.* Could mean far-hand in Latin. Or pompous wizard-guy.

Tenar – Priestess of the Tombs of Atuan, White Lady of Gont. Called *Arha* and *Goha* (in *The Tombs of Atuan*, *Tehanu*, *The Other Wind*). It's not an earth name, but it could be. See Tamar.

Terrence "Terry" McGinnis is Batman (or rather, one of them). This is a Roman family name and saint's name. Teren, a variant, is a hero in Mercedes Lackey's Valdemar books. Most people with this name go by Terry of course. Namesakes here include actress Terry Farrell (Dax) and authors Terry Goodkind, Terry Brooks, Terry Bisson, Terry Pratchett, and T.H. White. Terry Gilliam and Terry Jones were in *Monty Python* for a double reference. For characters, Terry Boot is a Ravenclaw student and member of Dumbledore's Army, while Terry Bellefleur is a beloved Iraq war veteran on *True Blood.* Apparently Terrys become writers and actors, good contributors to the community.

Thalia, meaning to flourish, is a heroine in *Percy Jackson.* She's named for one of the Greek Graces as well as the muse of song and dance.

Thayet is a heroine of Tamora Pierce's books. Exotic in that land, and more exotic in this one.

Theodore Nott, a Slytherin student in the same year as Harry Potter, can see Thestrals, but only makes a cameo appearance. Theodore "Teddy" Altman is Hulkling of the *Young Avengers.* See Ted.

Famed author Theodore Sturgeon (1918–1985) (itself

a pseudonym of Edward Hamilton Waldo) joins him for this classic name meaning "gift of God." Thea, Green Arrow's hero sister on *Arrow,* may be short for Theodora.

Theon Greyjoy might conceivably have a name that works on earth (though it's probably adapted from Theodore). Given that he's the unluckiest and most miserable character in their (admittedly unhappy) world, you might wanna rethink. Despite this, "The youngest of the Greyjoy clan – also known as Reek and tortured by Ramsay Bolton – is the most popular boys' name influenced by *Game of Thrones,* with 18 babies named after the character" (Poladian).

Theresa is the mother of Ender in *Ender's Game.* Theresa Cassidy is Siryn (daughter of Banshee) in *X-Men.* A different woman, called Tessa, is Sage. For a sweet and delightful heroine, Teresa "Tessa" Grey is the heroine of *The Infernal Devices* by Cassandra Clare. Tersa is the mad but brilliant heroine in *The Black Jewels Trilogy.* Teresa Agnes appears in *The Maze Runner.* The name is Greek for reaper (presumably the farm job, not the Grim version).

Theseus is a hero in *Percy Jackson* and *A Midsummer Night's Dream.* He's from Greek myth, though his home life after defeating the Minotaur was seriously disturbed.

Thessaly is the last of the witches of Thessaly in Neil Gaiman's *The Sandman.* Gaiman named this character after the land of witches in Greece.

Thomas is thoroughly loaded – and not just for William Thomas Riker. In real life, Thomas Patten Stafford was an astronaut on Gemini 6A, Gemini 9A, Apollo 10, and the Apollo-Soyuz Test Project, while Thomas Willis is known to be the Father of Neuroscience. Thomas Burnet was an English divine theologian and a notable writer on speculative cosmogony or the scientific theory of how the universe was created. Thomas Edison must be the most famous of the scientists.

Tom Welling stars on *Smallville,* while Tom Baker played the distinguished Fourth Doctor. Characters by this name are heroes in *The Maze Runner, Mighty Morphin Power Rangers, Verne's The Mysterious Island,* and *Pippi Longstocking* (for a truly esoteric collection). Tommy Clark/Nathan Bennet stars as chosen one in *Heroes Reborn.* Thomas "Tommy" Shepherd is Speed of the *Young Avengers.* Thomas Carnacki is a fictional occult detective. Tom Zarek is a complicated political prisoner and antihero on new *Battlestar Galactica.* Tom Paris is helmsman on *Star Trek: Voyager,* and Thomas Raith is Harry Dresden's half-brother in *The Dresden Files.* Beware! Tom Marvolo Riddle is the real name of Voldemort. Thom's a hero in *The Wheel of Time* and antihero in the Tamora Pierce's Alanna books.

Thor, a figure from Norse mythology, appears in the novel *The Restaurant at the End of the Universe* and in Marvel comics. He also appears in Neil Gaiman's *The Sandman* series. Buffy's actress also had a dog by this name. It may be better on a bodybuilder or pet than a child.

Thorin is the dwarf king in *The Hobbit.* Also the king of sour grapes.

Thrashbarg first appears in the novel *Mostly Harmless,* as a priest on Lamuella, the planet on which Arthur becomes the Sandwich-Maker. You wouldn't name the kid something a letter off from "trashbag," right?

Clone trooper Threepwood's name is a reference to Guybrush Threepwood, a character from the *Monkey Island* game series. Very dweeby.

Literary detective Thursday Next is the heroine of the

Thursday Next series. An awesome name, though maybe not for your kid.

Tiana the Disney princess (Greek for highest beauty) has undoubtedly gotten a post-movie boost in popularity. It might be short for Gratiana or Christiana. Tiana is voiced by Anika Noni Rose, for an alternative namesake.

Tiffany Aching is the beloved YA witch heroine of Discworld. It's Greek for "God's appearance," or so it looks. Another is the Bride of Chucky, however. One assumes they're both always ready for breakfast…

"Some call me…Tim" says the lightning-bolt flinging enchanter in *Monty Python and the Holy Grail.* Actor Tim Russ (Tuvok) and author Timothy Zahn (*Star Wars* novels) line up under this name. Timothy Hunter is a comic book sorcerer published by DC Comics, created by Neil Gaiman and John Bolton. The name means "honoring God," as Timothy was an apostle. Getting *Star Trek* and *Star Wars* in the same name likely deserves a bonus…five happy babies.

Titania is queen of fairyland in Shakespeare's *A Midsummer Night's Dream* and many fantasy novels including *Sandman* comics. Sounds really big. Titanic, even.

Titus stars in *Gormenghast* His name is Latin for saved or Greek for giant. The first seems to fit the character better. But talk about dysfunctional families!

Tomalak is a Romulan commander who sounds like an ancient throwing axe. Plus. totally made up.

Torak is a villainous god in the *Belgariad.* Sounds like a truly painful cough…

Tormund Giantsbane spends all his time in *Game of Thrones* bragging about his size. So if that's your goal here…

Tory Foster is the president's enigmatic assistant on new *Battlestar Galactica.* It could be short for many exotic things.

Touchstone (formerly Torrigan) is a prince in Garth Nix's *Abhorsen* series. While your child might be your touchstone, it seems best to keep these thoughts in your head, not on his birth certificate.

T'Pol…her outfit is so tight this might be short for the pole where she dances. Plus it's ethnic Vulcan, and you're likely not. Wouldn't want to offend the council or they'll make you duel to the death or something.

Tracy Caldwell Dyson was an astronaut on STS-118 and Soyuz TMA-18. Ptraci is a heroine in Terry Pratchett's Discworld. This fake Egyptian name earned lots of jokes (including references to author Pterry). Probably best to go with the normal Tracy spelling.

Travis Mayweather appears on *Enterprise* and Travis Touchdown in the game *No More Heroes.* Travis Stoll is a mischievous child of Hermes in *Percy Jackson.* It's English for "crossing," or possibly the guard at the toll booth. Not the most celebrated of jobs.

Trevor (belonging to the big farm") may be a nice name, Welsh for homestead, but it's also the geeky toad belonging to Neville Longbottom.

Trinity from *The Matrix* has a memorable name that's also devoutly Christian. And maybe you really like the number three. But surely you could go with Mary or a saint?

Tristan, a knight in Arthurian legend, has a tragic tragic life. Maybe because he was named this. Another rather sweet character stars in Gaiman's *Stardust.*

Trisha see Patricia

Tsu'tey from *Avatar* has a tasty name. Artificially foreign though.

Turonga Leela on *Futurama* is powerful, clever, and fun. Also sounds a bit hulking. Watch out for the one eye and giant purple ponytail.

Tuvok is so-named after his creators got sick of Vulcans with s-names. Otherwise, it's a Vulcan one-size-fits-all.

Tweedledum and Tweedledee. You gotta be kidding.

Twoflower is a tourist in Terry Pratchett's Discworld. Apparently our names sound just as strange to them.

Tycho Brahe was the famed Danish astronomer (1546-1601) named from the Greek Tyche, goddess of luck. Other characters are Tycho Celchu in the fictional *Star Wars* Universe. Brother-Captain Tycho appears in the *Warhammer* 40,000 universe and Tycho is the name of the desert ranger henchman from the computer game *Fallout.*

Tylendel is a hero in Mercedes Lackey's Valdemar books. Perhaps he's related to Tywin and Tyrion.

Tyrell is either the genius who created the Replicants in *Blade Runner* or the opportunist family of *Game of Thrones.*

Tyrion Lannister may be the best beloved figure in *Game of Thrones.* In 2014, 17 babies were named after him (Poladian). Tirian is a Narnia character, and Tyr is the perfect warrior of Gene Roddenberry's *Andromeda.* They may take their names from Tyr, the one-handed Norse god. All fighters of a sort, but none have the most happy lives. Other Tyr names like Tyrone are possible variants.

Tyro in *Avatar* has a nymph name. Neat.

Tyrone Johnson is the Marvel hero Cloak (of *Cloak and Dagger*, best known for the heroine's racy outfit). Another Tyrone is the nasty Count Rugen who studies torture on *The Princess Bride.* Lt. Col. Tyrus Cassius "T. C." McQueen (callsign "Queen 6") stars in *Space Above and Beyond.* It's Greek for king, always a powerful choice.

Neil deGrasse Tyson, an American astrophysicist and science communicator, has a name that's French for firebrand. Tyson is Percy Jackson's Cyclops brother. He's a nice guy, though do you want to be the one to tell your kid he's named for a slightly slow Cyclops?

Tywin Lannister is not a nice man. Surely Tyrion is a better *Game of Thrones* namesake. Though Tyrion killed both his parents…

Ulysses Paxton is a fictional character created by Edgar Rice Burroughs in his novel *The Master Mind of Mars.* The name also goes to a James Joyce character and of course the Greek mythological hero who has appeared on *Xena, Percy Jackson*, and many more fantasy epics. This is also the favorite poem of the commander of *Babylon 5.*

Æon Flux and her sister Una star in her action movie, while Una is the star (literally) in the film *Stardust.*

Certainly a one-of-a-kind name.

Unity Kinkaid is a heroine in *The Sandman.* Still, be cautious of those real-word names, especially strange ones.

Ursula, meaning bear, is the supervillainess of *The Little Mermaid,* a vampy octopus woman who may have ruined the name forever. Top science fiction author Ursula K. Le Guin was there first, however.

Valanice is the queen of *King's Quest,* though something of a damsel in distress.

Valda the Iron Maiden is a DC Comics heroine who actually dresses modestly. Surely that deserves a salute.

Valentine is the evil father of *The Moral Instruments,* and the loving sister of *Ender's Game.* The name, meaning "healthy," comes with a built-in holiday. Valentine is the nuanced sidekick of *Mirrormask.* Beka Valentine stars on *Andromeda.* Valentina Tereshkova was an astronaut on Vostok 6 and the first woman in space.

Dame Valerie Jane Goodall lends distinction to the name, though since no one knows this *is* her name, we're in obscure territory. It's French/Latin for Strong. Valère L'Envers is a lady in the Kushiel series by Jacqueline Carey. Valeria Meghan Richards is the supergenius daughter of the *Fantastic Four* couple. Valerie "Val" Cooper works with the X-Men, while in real life Valery Bykovsky was an astronaut on Vostok 5, Soyuz 22, Soyuz 31/29. Finally, Valerie is Miracle Max's wife in *The Princess Bride.* At least she claims she's not a witch. Valerian is a heroine in *Dragonslayer.* On the gender flip, Val Kilmer was in *Batman, Willow,* and much more.

Vána the Ever-young, goddess of Middle earth.

Admittedly, it's a Tolkien name you might get away with.

Vanessa Fisk is a Marvel Comics character, wife of supervillain Wilson Fisk. It means butterfly, a pretty name for a meanish lady. Vanessa Kapatelis is Silver Swan, a Wonder Woman supervillain. For a more positive reference, 1st Lt. Vanessa Damphousse (callsign "Ace of Hearts") stars in *Space Above and Beyond.*

Vanyel is a hero in Mercedes Lackey's *Valdemar* books. He's brave and clever despite his funny-name burden.

Varda, queen of stars in Middle Earth. Slightly more well-known than Vána, if you're trying to sneak in your Tolkien.

Varys: the conniving eunuch of *Game of Thrones.* C'mon – do you really want to name your kid for a conniving, semi-villainous eunuch? Really?

Vash the Stampede from *Trigun* is "the humanoid typhoon" since he always causes utter destruction, even while saving lives on the wild planet of Gunsmoke. Of course, Vash is also a *ST: TNG* bad girl. It's not clear if it's short for something. I guess you could make something up. Careful of the rhymes – brash, trash, hash, clash, stash.

Vastra: Victorian dinosaur lesbian crimefighting heroine of *Doctor Who.* Yes, really. Well, it's unusual. And she only eats bad guys…Two sad babies, just for being strange.

Veralidaine (Daine) is a shapeshifting heroine of Tamora Pierce's books. An exotic, clunky name that certainly *could* be real. But it's not.

Verence II of Lancre is a hero and somewhat runny

eyed king in Terry Pratchett's Discworld. It seems a variant on Terence.

Verna ("place of alder trees") is a heroine in *The Sword of Truth* by Terry Goodkind. She's an older nun, but incredibly brave and powerful. Her gender flip Vernon Dursley – Harry Potter's muggle uncle – is perfectly normal, thank you very much. And horrible.

Veronica Roth is the author of the popular *Divergent* series. The name means "bringer of victory." There's also Veronica from *Archie* comics.

Veruca Salt is the spoiled girl in *Charlie and the Chocolate Factory.* Terrible girl, terrible name. Though it does sound kinda credible.

Victor comes from victory of course. Characters include Viktor Krum Durmstrang student and Hermione's love interest, as well as one of Gale's little brothers in *The Hunger Games* and a male prostitute on *Dollhouse.* Vicky Austin is the heroine of the Austin family series of novels and stories by Madeleine L'Engle. Victor "Vic" Stone is superhero Cyborg, and X-Men Villain/Hero Sabertooth is Victor Creed. There's also Victor Von Doom (the *Fantastic Four* villain) and Victor Mancha, son of Ultron in Marvel's *Runaways.* Another stars in *Corpse Bride.*

From Roald Dahl's *Danny, Champion of the World.* Mr. Victor Hazell is the nasty, rich man that owned a lot of pheasants. His namesake may appear in *Despicable Me.* Victoria Hand works for SWORD in Marvel's universe. There's Vicki Donovan of *The Vampire Diaries.* Vicki and Victoria Waterfield were both early *Doctor Who* companions. Later came Vislor Turlough (the only traitor *Doctor Who* companion). Five happy babies and a good chance at a TARDIS.

Viggo Mortensen played Aragorn. Though that name with roots of "vigorous" and "son of death" certainly sounds fictitious.

Vin is the heroine of Brandon Sanderson's *Mistborn.* A clever, buttkicking heroine with all the superpowers. Though it does mean "wine" in English.

Vincent (romantic hero of *Beauty and the Beast*) shares a name with artist Vincent Van Gogh, Vincent the dog from *Lost*, and Vincent Valentine, the *Final Fantasy* character. It's French for Vincentius (conquering). There's also Vincent Crabbe, Jr. and Sr., disturbing Death Eaters.

Violante, also known as "her ugliness," is the daughter of the Adderhead and widow of Cosimo the Fair in *Inkheart.* The name probably means "violent" but "her ugliness" must be the deal breaker here.

Violet is for the purple flower, of course. Girl inventor Violet Baudelaire is a delightful main character of Lemony Snicket's *A Series of Unfortunate Events.* Other heroines include Violet Parr, from the movie *The Incredibles* and Violet Crawley, the Dowager Countess on *Downton Abbey.* Violet was a minor character on *Buffy the Vampire Slayer* and in *Harry Potter.* There's one in *American Horror Story.* But Violet Beauregarde chews gum all day in *Charlie and the Chocolate Factory* and comes to a sticky end.

Vir Cotto is an ordinary (alien) guy on *Babylon 5*. His name means man, and is also the root of words like "virile." Alien and yet very human and very macho. Unlike the character.

Virgil "Gus" Grissom was an astronaut on Mercury-Redstone 4 and Gemini 3 who died in the Apollo 1 fire. His name means "flourishing."

Virginia Lewis stars in *The 10th Kingdom* as a fairytale heroine. Virginia Apgar is best known for developing the Apgar Newborn Scoring System for determining health. Virginia Porcher is the heroine of a Madeleine L'Engle books. All heroines, but without a lot of dates.

Viserys Targaryen has an exotic, fantastical name in *Game of Thrones*. Then he dies with a bucket of melted gold poured on his head. Coincidence?

Vito Cornelius is the priest who assists Korben in *The Fifth Element*. It means lively. Or for a baby, squirmy.

Viviane is lady of the lake in some Arthurian mythos, including *The Mists of Avalon*. The name, related to vivacious, means full of life. Very nice, unless she discovers this character's a hooker in *Pretty Woman*.

Vizzini in *The Princess Bride* is a nasty troll of a person. And a murderer for hire. And shouts "inconceivable" a lot. All serious deal-breakers.

Voldemort's name means "death wish." Where do all the villains get these evil cognates?

Vroomfondel may or may not be a philosopher in *Hitchhiker's Guide*. Your kid may or may not hate you…

King Vultan leads the Hawkmen in *Flash Gordon*. And sounds like something you use to oil your car.

Wade Wilson is Deadpool, a wisecracking Marvel antihero fast gaining popularity. And a film. He'll be good at crossing water, as per the name meaning.

Wallace is a *Pokémon* character. It means foreigner or

Welshman. Wallace & Gromit are beloved claymation heroes with a cheese fixation. Meanwhile, Wallace Shawn goes around *The Princess Bride* shouting "Inconceivable!" and also played the Grand Nagus on *Star Trek*. In the latter case, are you imagining your child is a greedy joke of a character? If you choose to use the name "Wallace," make sure it means what you think it means.

Walter Koenig, who played Chekov on *Star Trek* and the villain Bester on *Babylon 5* is a fun scifi namesake. There's also Dr. Walter Bishop (*Fringe*) and Walter Skinner from *The X-Files*. Walter M. Schirra, Jr. commanded Apollo 7 and R. Walter Cunningham was an astronaut on Apollo 7. For a painful variant, Walder Frey is a villain in *Game of Thrones* and Walder is the real name of village idiot Hodor. Wally West is the Flash (or one of them). If you're trying to be oh so clever and obscure, you could name your kid Wally for Wall-E. I guess. If you must.

Wanda Maximoff is Scarlet Witch – one of the early butt-kicking Avengers who wields inconceivable destruction. She does have a substantial dark side though. The name is German for "family" or "wanderer."

Warren Kenneth Worthington III is Angel in *X-Men*, while Warren Meers is a nasty villain on *Buffy*. One's pompous and one's evil, but the name itself seems okay. For "animal enclosure," at least.

Warwick Davis played Wicket the Ewok, the title character in 1998's *Willow,* the evil sprite in the *Leprechaun* movies, and Professor Flitwick in the *Harry Potter* films. Obviously he's named for a place in England.

Wayoun is an amoral alien clone on *DS9*. Waaaay out there as a name.

Wedge Antilles flies an x-wing on *Star Wars.* Not precisely a name though.

Wednesday, for the *Addams Family* daughter, seems rather goth to the point of cruelty. However, some American parents go for it. "The name grew in popularity throughout the 1990s, although the best year for Wednesday was 2013" (MooseRoots). Do you want your kid wandering around with that creepy stare while everyone treats her like a freak? I thought not. She would be a champion finger snapper, however.

Weena is the futuristic heroine of *The Time Machine.* Sweet and airheaded, but it appears her tribe don't have the brains to tease her for her name.

Wendy was a name made up by the author of *Peter Pan*, but it really, really caught on. Also, Wendy Lawrence was an astronaut on four missions. Either way, she'll be able to fly.

Werner Heisenberg is noted for his crucial contributions to quantum mechanics. Kids may have called him a wiener though.

Wesley is an English name, meaning "western meadow." There's whiny supergenius Wesley Crusher of *Star Trek* who later becomes a hero, ridiculously pompous Wesley Wyndam-Pryce of *Buffy* and *Angel* who *also* later becomes a hero, and the farmboy of *The Princess Bride* who finally…you see where this is going. Also, Wesley Dodds is the original Sandman in *The Sandman* and DC comics, and Wes Janson is a fighter pilot and founding member of the elite Rogue Squadron in the *Star Wars* universe. Some interesting fantasy connections, though the kid will be burdened with some very obvious fantasy staples.

Weston (English for "West Town," unsurprisingly) wants to colonize and mine gold on Mars in the C.S. Lewis books. Well, someone should. Why not your kid?

Whoopi Goldberg played many beloved characters, most notably space bartender Guinan. The name seems terribly teasable, however. Do you know what making whoopee is?

Wilbur is German for resolute. Wilbur and Orville Wright invented the airplane, though Wilbur the pig must get a nod as well.

Wilfred Mott is a beloved elderly *Doctor Who* companion. His name is Germanic for "will" and "peace."

Wilhelmina Benedict is a heroine in *The Black Jewels Trilogy,* while Wilhelmina Grubbly-Plank is the substitute Care of Magical Creatures professor. This is also the name of the heroine of *Dracula.* See Mina

"Danger, Will Robinson!" William, a widespread name from the German, means "resolute protector." It's adored in the Whedonverse, belonging to Willow/William Pratt/ Liam/ Ben Wilkinson/Richard Wilkins III/Carl William Kraft/ Billy (*Doctor Horrible*) Also Billy Fordham ("Lie to Me"), Billy Palmer ("Nightmares"), Billy Crandal ("I Only Have Eyes For You"), Billy ("Billy"), Billy Lane (*Welcome to the Team*), and Willy the Snitch.

Actors include William Shatner, Wil Wheaton, Billy Dee Williams, Bill Nye "The Science Guy," William Hartnell (First Doctor), and Billy Boyd (Pippin Took). There are authors William Gibson and William Morrison. William A. Anders was an astronaut on Apollo 8. William C. McCool died on the Columbia.

In children's fantasy, Will Stanton is the young hero of *The Dark is Rising* while Will Parry takes a similar role in the *Golden Compass* series. William "Billy" Kaplan is Wiccan of the *Young Avengers.* Other characters include Will Turner and Bootstrap Bill from *Pirates of the Caribbean,* William Riker, Willy Wonka, Rory Williams (*Doctor Who* companion), Ron's brother Bill Weasley, Capt. William "Buck" Rogers of *Buck Rogers in the 25th Century,* and William from the *Ender's Game* series. Billy Cranston is a Mighty Morphin Power Ranger. Jim Nightshade and William Halloway star in Bradbury's "Something Wicked This Way Comes." Billy Batson is the superhero Captain Marvel and Bill Compton is a romantic lead on *True Blood.* Billie Jenkins is a young charge for Paige on *Charmed.* William de Worde is a hero in Terry Pratchett's Discworld. William Adama is commander on new *Battlestar Galactica,* where Billy Keikeya is a shy hero. For a gender flip, Wilma Deering is the heroine of *Buck Rogers in the 25th Century.*

Willow Rosenberg's namesake, the willow tree, is graceful and feminine. The word "wiccan" may come from this tree. The willow is a tree of inspiration, intuition, and dream, fitting for the *Buffy* heroine and witch. She shares this with the hero of the eighties film *Willow.* Lisa Milbrand wrote in *Parents Magazine*: "The nature name Joss chose for Buffy's geek-chic best friend (and future most-powerful-witch-in-the-universe) was barely in the top 1000 when the show started, and now is continuing its rise, currently ranking as the 171st most popular name for girls in the U.S. (You can also thank Will and Jada Smith, who picked it for their daughter during this same timeframe.)"

Winifred "Fred" Burkle is a heroine on *Angel.* It's is an old-fashioned countrified name, though Fred or Freddie is more modern (Winnie is less likely nowadays). In Welsh, it means "blessed peacemaking," which is her role on the show. Winifred, the star of *Hocus Pocus,* scares children and is hilarious to adults. The name took a dip in popularity in

1994, but has trended upward since 2010 (MooseRoots).

Winston means "wine's town" a less-distinguished name for the savior of Britain, Winston Churchill. The name is shared by Winston Smith, hero of *1984*, and a character in *The Maze Runner*

Winter Musgrave stars in Marion Zimmer Bradley's *Witchlight*, while another Winter is dystopian cyberpunk Snow White in Marissa Meyer's fairytale series. A chilly name for cold, damaged heroines.

Worf. Seriously?

Xaphania ("The Lord is my secret") is a heroine of the *Golden Compass* series. She's quite a mouthful.

Shape-shifting alien Xavin is a hero and love interest in Marvel's *Runaways*. It's from Xavier, Basque for "owner of a new house." Well if the kid xaves up…

Xayide is the bad seductive lady in *The Neverending Story* (book and second movie). Her bad attitude must derive from spelling and pronunciation pain.

Xena kicked butts through the nineties and defined barbarian girl power. But do you really want to do that to a little baby? Think of the war cries.

Xenophilius Lovegood is father of Luna Lovegood and editor of *The Quibbler*. Based on the Latin, it means "lover of foreign things." Nice sentiment, awkward name.

Yavanna, nature goddess of Middle Earth, will certainly stir things up.

Ygraine, or Igraine, is the mother of King Arthur.

Most famous for sleeping with the wrong man and begetting him. Yvaine is a star in *Stardust*.

Ygritte is the hot red-haired barbarian of *Game of Thrones*. Keep in mind all the stripping scenes on the show, combined with her final fate…If you're thinking of this one, you know nothing.

Ylla, a Martian woman trapped in an unromantic marriage in Bradbury's *Martian Chronicles* must struggle with her alien name. Y'll understand.

Yolanda Montez (Wildcat) is a DC superhero, and *Firefly* bad girl Saffron goes by that name at one point. It means Violet. See Violet

Yooden Vranx is the late former President of the Galaxy, the direct predecessor to Zaphod Beeblebrox in *Hitchhiker's Guide*. Seems they hand out power alphabetically.

Ysabell, Duchess of Sto Helit, is a heroine in Terry Pratchett's Discworld. She's a fun hero, but Isabelle is more standard.

Ysandre de la Courcel is the queen in the *Kushiel* series by Jacqueline Carey. Her name is Greek for liberator. Certainly, it's freeingly original.

Zacharias Smith is a Hufflepuff student who deserted before the Battle of Hogwarts. Zack Allan is an everyman hero on *Babylon 5*. Zechariah Morgan is an American boy, mentioned in the *Ender's Game* novella, *A War of Gifts*. Zachary Gray is a romantic interest in some of Madeleine L'Engle's books. This Bible name means "Remembered by God." That's nice, but the kid may not be remembered when the class hands out cupcakes alphabetically.

Zaphod Beeblebrox in *Hitchhiker's Guide* is president of the galaxy. Where could you go wrong?

Zatanna is a DC magician superhero. Perhaps she's related to Zan of the Wonder Twins…

Zathras is an alien on *Babylon 5*. Like him, you could have a bunch of siblings all named Zathras with slight differences in pronunciation.

Lord Zedd is a villain in *Mighty Morphin Power Rangers*. Seems he's the end of everything.

Zeddicus Zu'l "Zedd" Zorander from Goodkind's *Sword of Truth* series has a very alliterative name. This is likely the best that can be said of it.

Zelda stars in many computer games and a short-lived eighties television show. She has her butt-kicking princess side, much like Zelda Fitzgerald. Zelda Heap is a character in the *Septimus Heap* book series and Zelda is Sabrina's aunt on *Sabrina the Teenage Witch*. The name is a nickname for Griselda, "dark battle," and also the feminine form of the Yiddish name Selig, meaning "blessed," or "happy." Surely the latter would be better for the child.

Zelena is the Wicked Witch of the West in *Once Upon a Time*. For some reason.

Zemenar heads the Society of Wizards in Patricia C. Wrede's *Enchanted Forest Chronicles*. Each time, he's beaten and practically yells "curses, foiled again!" in his hokiness.

Zephram Cochrane invented warp drive and takes his name from the mythic Zephyr, the West Wind. Kind of a rebellious drunk in the film though.

Zhora is a powerful replicant on *Blade Runner*. With a science-fictiony name. Are you zure?

Zia Rashid is a fire magician and romantic lead in Rick Riordan's *The Kane Chronicles*. The name is Biblical for sweat or swelling, which seems just a little cruel.

As a name that spans the genres, Zoe is the amazing warrior of *Firefly*. Zoe Heriot is a beloved *Doctor Who* companion, and Zoe Graystone stars on *Caprica,* though she becomes a cyborg. Actress Zoe Saldana stars in *Avatar*. There's also a couple in *Percy Jackson* and *Being Human* (US). #7 in 2014. The name means "life" as a variant on Eve…though she'll be picked last in the alphabet. See Eve

Zoidberg from *Futurama* is an alien lobster and the butt of every joke. Make sure your child is neither of these.

Zo'or on *Earth: Final Conflict* is a villain with a name that sounds like the Heimlich maneuver. Ugh.

Ethnic Names

Sometimes scifi writers choose ethnic names. Generally these are *very* ethnic, to emphasize a multicultural world. *Star Trek* for instance, brought in Japanese Hikaru Sulu and Keiko O'Brien as well as Pavel Chekhov from Russia and Nyota Uhura from Africa. All these names strongly indicate their background. *Ender's Game* is likewise a multicultural alliance, with names to reflect it. The catch is that the authors, generally American, will make up plausible names, or use the most direct (J.K. Rowling named her Indian students for the goddesses of courage and wisdom, then placed them in Gryffindor and Ravenclaw). Often these authors default to the obvious, but for those who would like to combine an Indian or Chinese name with scifi, you're in the right place.

African

Aisha is Arabic for woman and Swahili for life. She's the wife of Mohammad and also a Power Ranger.

Asajj Ventress is Count Dooku's newest Darth and commander of the droid army during the Clone Wars Asaju, its closest equivalent, is a Nigerian surname.

Barack means "blessed." See Barak.

Chi Cho was a Pantoran male and Chairman of the Pantoran Assembly during *Star Wars'* Clone Wars. Chi references everyone's personal spiritual guardian in Igbo.

Ghanima, from Swahili origins, means good fortune. She's the daughter of Paul and Chani, heroes of *Dune.*

Jeneta and her father Mmadukaaku star in *Libriomancer*. In fact, Jeneta (from Janet) is a precocious teen and gifted magician. Her father's name means "Humans are better than wealth," a sentiment he shows.

Jiwe, middle name of DC superheroine Mari Jiwe McCabe, also known as Vixen, is Swahili for stone. She's certainly strong enough.

Mowgli is from *The Jungle Book*. But everyone knows this. Kipling claimed it meant "frog," but he wasn't a language master…

Nala appears in African languages as "successful or beloved." In Disney, literally a lioness. Also, Nala See was a female Kaminoan (white, tall necked alien from *Attack of the Clones*) who worked out of the Republic's secret medical center during the Clone Wars.

Nyota is a Swahili name for girls meaning "star." It's semi-canon that this was Lt. Uhura's first name.

Simba is, appropriately, Swahili for lion.

Sineya, the name is given to the First Slayer of *Buffy*, references a region in Kouroussa, Guinea. She's thus associated with the land and the dawn of civilization.

"Uhura" comes from the Swahili word uhuru, "freedom." Nichelle Nichols states in her book *Beyond Uhura* that the name was inspired by her having had with her a copy of Robert Ruark's book *Uhuru* on the day she read for the part.

Zuko from *Avatar* means "harmony." Of course, he'll have to come to peace with his place in the alphabet.

Arabic

Aayla Secura was a Twi'lek Jedi Knight during the Clone Wars. Certainly an alphabetical advantage. The Arabic name Aaliyah means "sublime." Ayla is a common name in Turkish, meaning "halo of light around the moon." There's one in *Clan of the Cave Bear.*

Ahmed, meaning "more commendable" in Arabic, appears in the *Ender's Game* series. Ahmed Hassan Zewail is an Egyptian scientist who won the Nobel Prize in Chemistry in 1999, known to be the Father of femtochemistry because of his innovation in Physical Chemistry. Achmed the Mad/Achmed the 'I Just Get These Headaches' and 71-Hour Ahmed are characters in Terry Pratchett's Discworld.

We all know where Aladdin is from…

Alia is the precocious psychic child of *Dune.* The word *Aliyah* means to go up and make a pilgrimage. As a name, Alia is the feminine form of Ali, meaning High or Exalted, one of the 99 attributes of Allah. This is also Aladdin's alias in the Disney movie and the hero of Ali Baba. Alai, one of Ender's best friends from the *Ender's Game* series is likely related.

Altair is the brightest star in the constellation Aquila. Also, Altair Ibn-La'Ahad is the protagonist in the video game *Assassin's Creed.*

Amir Amr, Amhar, Anir, and Amir are all names for King Arthur's son. Arabic or Hebrew, it means prince. For added geek points, Amir Bagheri is an Iranian chess grandmaster. Amira is the feminine form, appearing in *EastEnders* and *Veronica Mars* as well as lending its name to a software platform. #212 in the US.

Anaheed is one of Buffy Summers' roommates in San Francisco in the season nine comics. Armenian for "immaculate."

Princess Cassima is a love interest in *King's Quest* 6, though something of a damsel in distress. Her name appears to come from Qasim, "one who divides goods among his people." Good trait in a ruler, and this name will blend in the US.

See Dara

Farid "unique" is a boy from Ali Baba read into life in *Inkheart.* An endearing young hero.

Jasper, Persian for keeper of treasure, is one of the *Twilight* vampires. You've been warned.

Jehan, Muslim for "the World," is Dustfinger's child in the children's novel *Inkheart.*

Kamala, "perfection," is the new Ms. Marvel and a beloved teen heroine. Yes, after you read the comics, this name will seem like perfection too. It's also a Hindi name meaning "she of the lotus." Kamala is one of the Ten Mahavidyas, the wisdom Goddesses.

Karima Shapandar is Omega Sentinel in *X-Men.* The name is Arabic for friend. Plus, superhero.

Majel Barrett Rodenberry played many *Star Trek* characters, most memorably the computer voice through several shows. The name is Arabic for beautiful, but unusual in the US.

Muhammad ibn Musa al-Khwarizmi was a Persian mathematician, astronomer, astrologer geographer and scholar from around 780. Mohammad Abdus Salam, from the twentieth century, was a Pakistani theoretical physicist and astrophysicist, as well as the first Pakistani and Muslim to win the Nobel laureate in Physics for his work in Electro-Weak Theory. The name of course salutes the founder of the Muslim religion, meaning "glorified."

Naawat is a crow hero-trickster in Tamora Pierce's Tortall books. Naawat is a crow hero-trickster in Tamora Pierce's Tortall books. Arabic for core.

Nevtiri stars in *Avatar.* Her name is related to the Egyptian word for nature.

Omar Khayyam was one of the major mathematicians and astronomers of the medieval period. He did impressive work in algebra, though he's also known for his poetry and the line "A jug of wine, a loaf of bread, and thou." There's also actor Omar Sharif, while Omar Toggs was a Rodian bounty hunter during the Clone Wars. The name means "eloquent."

Rabastan Lestrange is a Death Eater, brother of Rodolphus Lestrange This name may be a play on Rastaban, the traditional name of one of the stars of the constellation Draco. It's Arabic for "Head of the serpent." Definitely a bad guy name.

Ra's al Ghul is a DC comics villain. Ras Thavas is a mad scientist created by Edgar Rice Burroughs in his 1927 novel *The Master Mind of Mars.* The name means "leader," but these are bad ones.

Sazed is a hero of Brandon Sanderson's *Mistborn.* It means "royalty," and indeed, he has a great destiny. Perhaps your kid will too.

Shameer ("stone") is a character in *The Elder Scrolls* and the genie in *King's Quest* 6.

Sayid Jarrah (from *Lost*) has a name that means "master." Powerful stuff.

Sooraya is the X-Man Dust. Her name means "bright light" and is related to that of Princess Soraya, wife of the last Shah of Iran.

Yasmin see Jasmine

Zaheer ("helper") is the leader of the Red Lotus in *Legend of Korra.* He reaches enlightenment, and, as an airbender, he learns to fly. Always a suitable goal.

Chinese

Aang means "peaceful soaring" and is a reulctant hero and pacifist in *Avatar: The Last Airbender.*

Bolin in *The Legend of Korra* is a heroic earthbender with great family loyalty. The name has a Chinese origin meaning "rain."

Cho Chang is a Ravenclaw student and Harry Potter's love interest. Her name meaning is unclear, though it's a Japanese unit of measurement.

Chun-Li is the warrior babe in the game *Street Fighter.* Her name means "beautiful spring," but she's a bit too memorable as a character.

Fang Zar is a senator during the Clone Wars. "Fang" means square in Chinese.

Huyang: Chinese surname that means "Yellow."

Professor Huyang was a droid who served the Jedi Order as a Lightsaber expert during the Clone Wars.

Iroh in *Avatar: The Last Airbender,* also known as "The Dragon of the West," is a Firebending master and former heir to the Fire Nation throne. It comes from a Mandarin word meaning old or beautiful river.

Jiaying is a Chinese name for girls meaning household flourishing. Also a powerful matriarch and Inhuman on *Agents of SHIELD.*

Jin Kwon hails from *Lost,* while there's a Jinora in *Avatar.* It may come from Chinese words meaning gold, bright or embroidered; and graceful. All lovely.

Joss Whedon self-named, and his name is Chinese for lucky.

Katara, also called Kya, in *Avatar: The Last Airbender* is Aang's best friend and eventual girlfriend. Characters perplexingly mean "block," "pagoda," and "pull."

Lin Beifong is the Chief of Police of the Republic City Police Department in *Avatar: The Last Airbender.* Hers is a common Chinese surname.

Liu Yang was the first Chinese woman in space. Another surname.

Melinda Qiaolian "The Cavalry" May is the disciplined warrior on *Agents of SHIELD.* The middle name means "always skillful," which she is.

Shang-Chi ("rising of the spirit") is a Marvel Comics character, often called the "Master of Kung Fu."

Shen from the *Ender's Game* series has a name that means "Deep Thought." Extra scifi points from *Hitchhiker's Guide.*

Sun Kwon (*Lost*) shares a name with an entire family from *Dragon Ball* as well as Soon Kim – a character in the webcomic *Order of the Stick*. Sun is a translation of a common Chinese surname, referencing many place names and historical figures.

Toph Beifong is a blind Earthbending grandmaster of the Earth Kingdom in *Avatar: The Last Airbender*. The name means "expanding hibiscus."

Wan in *Avatar* has a Mandarin name meaning gentle or gracious. Very nice.

Wu from the *Ender's Game* series has the name of emperors. Fitting for his role in the story, it means "martial." Woo.

Xi'an "Shan" Coy Mahn is Karma (X-Men). Her name, fittingly, means "Western peace." Or perhaps "alphabetically disadvantaged."

Yi So-yeon of South Korea was an astronaut on Soyuz TMA-12/11. Her name is Chinese for "suitable, just, firm, joy, harmony, ceremony." A very pretty range.

Yue in *Avatar* is Chinese for moon. You may have a rough time with this in America, though.

Zhao in *Avatar* has a name that means "above and beyond all." Quite powerful and all-encompassing.

Prince Zuko, later Fire Lord Zuko, is the primary villain in *Avatar: The Last Airbender*. His name means "loved one" or "failure." Obviously, you should lean toward the former if choosing this one.

Japanese

Many anime names are formed with two-word Kanji, to form a double word name…though without the Japanese characters, the actual meanings can vary.

Akane, Japanese for red madder dye, is found in the anime and manga series *Soul Eater.* It's popular across similar series, including *Angel Tales, Pokémon, Pani Poni, Higurashi no Naku Koro ni, Cross Game, Ranma ½,* and the *Tales of the Otori* series by Lian Hearn.

Akira is a unisex name, Japanese for bright. It hails from the popular anime of this name.

Ami "second beauty" Mizuno is Sailor Mercury in *Sailor Moon.*

Ando, Japanese for "peaceful east" or "peaceful wisteria," lends its name to Ando Masahashi (*Heroes*).

Asami in *The Legend of Korra* has a Japanese name meaning "morning beauty."

Asuka Langley Soryu from *Neon Genesis Evangelion* trained to be an Eva pilot until her mother went mad and killed herself, leaving Asuka traumatized and toying with her own insanity. It means, appropriately, "flying like a bird." A heroine, but a damaged one.

Chiaki Mukai, M.D. of Japan was an astronaut on STS-65 and STS-95. Her name varyingly means "thousand lights" "thousand autumns," or "shining wisdom." All very pretty.

Eikichi Onizuka is a street-wise teacher to the point of being more than a little gangster. His name likely means "supremely fortunate." Certainly, he's lucky in his many child disciples.

Goku stands out in *Dragon Ball Z* as the deep-down hero and strongest man in the world. "Go" means enlightenment, and "Ku" means Sky or Emptiness. The name is also a pun on a vegetable, for those who want to go corny.

Hachiman Hikigaya from anime takes his name from the divinity of archery and war. This risks significant mayhem in his future and yours.

Haru is a uinisex name meaning sunlight, which appears in *Rave Master.*

Haruhi Fujioka first appeared in *Ouran High School Host Club,* 2006. She's a powerful tomboy heroine whose name means "spring day." *The Melancholy of Haruhi Suzumiya* is another source.

With Vespa scooter and Rickenbacker bass guitar, Haruko Haruhara of *FLCL* is fun, crude, and often crazy. Spring-child or Sunlight-child.

Hiro from *Soul Eater* shares a name with Hiro Nakamura (*Heroes*) and Hiro Hiyorimi, a protagonist of *Princess Resurrection.* This is also Keiko O'Brien's father and a giant ninja toad in *Naruto.* Generally meaning "abundant, prosperous," its most famous holder may be Hiro Mashima, Japanese manga artist and the creator of *Rave Master* and *Fairy Tail.* Might want to delay a while on mentioning the ninja toad namesake.

Hikaru Sulu helped make the original *Star Trek*

multinational. His unisex name means "shining." A near-countless list of fictional characters share it, hailing from *Princess Ai, Parodius, Ouran High School Host Club,* and more.

Hisako Ichiki is Armor of the X-Men, a fierce young woman invented by Joss Whedon. She shares her name with the Princess Takamado of Japan, several actresses, the avenger ghost character of *Killer Instinct,* and the guitarist of Girls Dead Monster in the anime *Angel Beats!* The name means "enduring child."

Hoshi Sato is the translator on *Star Trek: Enterprise.* Her name, appropriately for sci-fi, means "star."

Ichigo Kurosaki hails from *Bleach*, while Ichigo Hoshimiya is the protagonist of *Aikatsu,* and a student of Starlight Academy. It means one enlightenment or strawberry.

Ikki in *Avatar* means one horse. Two horses seems better…

Kakashi Hatake from *Naruto* actually beats the hero in popularity polls. With his angst-filled past, he could give the hot vampires serious competition. This is also the name of a prince in *Howl's Moving Castle* who is temporarily transformed int a scarecrow. In fact, the two-part name literally means scare-crow. Seems a mean name, even if the child is rather unkempt.

Kamina, from anime, means "child of love." How sweet. It's not American, but it could be.

Kazuto Kirigaya, Kazuto Hongō, and Kazuto Izuka all are fictional heroes in visual novels and anime/manga. It means "harmonious person." Guess that's their secret.

Keiko O'Brien of *Star Trek* has a name that may mean "blessed child," "respectful child," or "open-eyed child." All good things. She shares this with Keiko Onuki or Keiko Inoue in *Battle Royale* and Keiko Yukimura of *YuYu Hakusho.*

Kenshin Himura of *Ruroni Kenshin* is a killer sworn to peace – a great contradiction. His name, fittingly, means "modest truth."

After Earth stars Jaden Smith as Kitai Raige. Kitai means anticipation or hope – lovely, but with a touch of the feline.

Kwannon is related to the Buddhist goddess of mercy, Guanyin. Also the name of X-Man Revanche.

Keiko O'Brien's baby Kiriyoshi is likely from Kyoshi, "pure" or "quiet" in Japanese. Kyoshi appears in *Avatar.*

Lain Iwakura of *Serial Experiments* starts off very juvenile, wearing a full body teddy bear suit. However, when she discovers the world of The Wired, she becomes powerful, confident, and terrible.

Maka from the anime and manga series *Soul Eater* comes from Mika, beautiful perfume or increase.

Mako in *Avatar* means "child of truth." He was named in honor of actor Mako Iwamatsu who voiced Uncle Iroh in *The Last Airbender.*

Makoto Kino is Sailor Jupiter. It means "sincerity."

Mamoru Chiba is Tuxedo Mask in *Sailor Moon.* Appropriately, it means protector.

Mikasa Ackerman is a beloved character in *Attack on Titan* and a mountain in Nara. This also corresponds to the Spanish "Mi casa es su casa," and may lead to teasing.

Heroes Reborn stars Miko Otomo, Katana Girl. It's from Mikoto (beautiful harp, beautiful truth).

See Mina

Minako Aino is Sailor Venus. Her name means "beautiful apple tree child."

Motoko Kusanagi of *Ghost in the Shell* is a feminist detective, clever and capable. Of course, she's also trapped in an artificial body. Her name means origin-child or child of the source. Aren't we all.

Natsu ("summer") Dragneel is a mage of the *Fairy Tail* Guild.

Ozai in *Avatar* is named from Japanese words meaning "great wealth." Always good to have a plan.

Rei Hino is Sailor Mars. It means lovely bell or the tinkling of jade.

Rika "true fragrance" hails from *Higurashi no Naka Koro Ni*. Bet she smells good.

Roku "ensoulment" sounds sufficiently fantastical and appears in *Avatar*.

Sai from *Naruto* has a unisex name, meaning "talented."

Sakura, "cherry blossom," is another name from *Naruto*.

Satsu is Buffy's girlfriend in the comics. It means killer, emphasizing that she was predestined to be a Slayer.

Senshi is Japanese for "warrior," "guardian," or "fighter." Zoë Kravitz plays Senshi Raige in *After Earth*. SailorSenshi is a fictional group of heroines from the *Sailor Moon* franchise.

Shinji ("second son") Ikari of *Neon Genesis Evangelion* is a whiny adolescent comparable to Wesley Crusher who lives the teen experience. Is this your goal?

Shiro Yoshida, Sunfire of the X-Men, means "Samurai," appropriate for a warrior.

Sokka in *Avatar: The Last Airbender* has a name meaning "I understand." Certainly something you want to see in a kid.

Suki is the leader of the exclusively female Kyoshi Warriors in the *Avatar* universe. It's Japanese for "beloved." See Sookie.

Taiga means any number of two-word combinations from big river to peaceful spear to fat congratulations to great elegance It might be best to discover which, or you could pick your own. Taiga Aisaka is a popular *Toradora* character and there's also an actor by this name. Japanese painter and calligrapher Ike no Taiga joins the list.

Tamika ("people") is a character in *The Elder Scrolls*. Not much distinction there.

Toshiko Sato is the tech genius of *Torchwood*. This name can mean "intelligent child," "superior child," "child of the year" or "child of the season." This first seems to apply best to the character.

Tsubaki ("camellia") from the anime and manga series *Soul Eater* has a pretty floral name.

Ukichiro Nakaya is known for having created the very first artificial snowflakes.

Usagi Tsukino is Sailor Moon. Her name, sweetly, means "rabbit of the moon." Nibble nibble.

Vegeta of *Dragon Ball Z* is a twisty bad guy who finally finds redemption. He's clearly stuck with the ultimate vegetative name.

Yuki means "happiness" or "snow." Lovely, unless American kids pronounce it yucky. This unisex name appears in *The Melancholy of Haruhi Suzumiya* and *Fruits Basket.*

Other Asian

Appa is Aang's flying bison and spirit companion in *Avatar: The Last Airbender.* "Appa" in Tamil and Korean is similar to a word that means "father."

See Dara

Mai in *Avatar* has a name that's Japanese for dance, Chinese for elegance, and Vietnamese for cherry blossom.

Melaka Fray is Joss Whedon's future slayer in his comic books. Melaka is a place name in Malaysia – both Malacca Town and the Melaka or Malacca River. The name comes from the fruit-bearing Malacca tree.

Momo is the only known winged lemur in *The Legend*

of Korra. Chinese for furry or Japanese for "peach." Momo is also short for the Japanese dwarf flying squirrel "Momonga." More for a pet than a person, no matter how cuddly.

Pabu is a mischievous male fire ferret who belongs to Bolin in *The Legend of Korra.* In Korean, Pabu is a term of endearment that can also mean "silly you." In Tibetan, it means "puffball." Also seems better for pets.

Pema in *Avatar* has a Tibetan origin meaning lotus, often specifically Buddah's lotus.

Suriyawong from the *Ender's Game* series has a Thai name, meaning uncertain.

Tenzin is the youngest child of Avatar Aang and Katara and the oldest living airbending master. It's from the Tibetan Bstan-'dzin – "upholder of teachings."

Ty-lee in *Avatar* is Taiwanese for calm and beautiful. Very serene.

Indian

The traditional Hindi name Akbar (That's Admiral Ackbar, soldier!) is on a steep downward decline, with just nine boys born with the name in the U.S. in 2014 (Holeman). As Admiral Ackbar, this one is clearly recognizable as the fish-man from *Star Wars.* Don't let your cat get the wrong idea!

Aouda, heroine from *Around the World in Eighty Days,* has a name that may mean princess. Or "she of many vowels."

Princess Azula is Zuko's sister and a major antagonist in *Avatar.* She is likely named for the Spanish word for blue, "azul," or the Hindi word for demon. Probably best to make sure before naming your kid this.

See Balin

Bolin from *Avatar* has an Indian name meaning orator.

Bumi in *Avatar* has a name that means "earth" in Sanskrit. In fact, he's the crazy genius king of an earth kingdom.

Chani, wife of the *Dune* protagonist Paul, is Sanskrit for chickpea. Little and cute, or a healthy snack.

Hiya or "She-who-must-be-obeyed," stars in the novel *She*. The name is sweet, meaning "heart," but she's an intimidating figure.

King Kala, ruler of the Shark Men in *Flash Gordon,* shares a name with Kala, the ape who raises Tarzan. For nonanimalistic namesakes, there's Kala, Queen of the Netherworld in Marvel Comics, and Kala Dandekar, a character on *Sense8*. They are named for Kala Ratri, one of nine forms of the Hindu goddess Parvati or Shakti. The name means "time."

Kalpana Chawla of India and the US was an astronaut on STS-87 and STS-107, then died on the crash of the Columbia. Along with her heroism, this name actually means "fantasy."

Kaneka is a heroine in the *Kushiel* series by Jacqueline Carey. Kanika means atom, seed or gold in Hindi. Lovely choices, with a name that works across countries.

Kavita Rao is a doctor who works with the X-Men, invented by Joss Whedon. She may be related to his Dr.

Rao on *Serenity*. In Sanskrit, Kavita means poem. Charming.

British Indian actor Kunal Nayyar plays Rajesh from *The Big Bang Theory*. The name Kunal means lotus or "bird with the beautiful eyes." How pretty!

Kuvira "courageous woman" is a master earthbender and metalbender in *Avatar: The Last Airbender*. Quite versatile, this character is both the captain of the city's guard and part of a dance troupe.

See Maya

See Mina

Mohinder Suresh (*Heroes*) has a name that means "great rain or thunder god." Powerful stuff.

Nagini is a snake belonging to Lord Voldemort. The word means snake in Hindi, and also appears in *Rikki Tikki Tavi*. Both times, she's a bad guy. More oddly, Naga is a female polar bear dog that belongs to Avatar Korra as her animal guide and spirit companion in *The Legend of Korra*.

Nidhi Shah stars in the *Libriomancer* series by Jim C. Hines. Her name references one of the nine treasures (nawanidhi) belonging to Kuvera, the god of wealth.

Padma Patil, member of Dumbledore's Army, attends the Yule Ball with Harry Potter. She's a Ravenclaw, appropriately named for the Indian goddess of wisdom.

14 girls were named Padme, Sanskirt for lotus, in 2014 – clearly, the name has become more popular since the release of *Revenge of the Sith* in 2005 (Holeman). Do the

namers remember she died in that one?

Parvati Patil is a Gryffindor student in Harry's year, an identical twin sister who's named for the Indian goddess of courage.

Rajesh from *The Big Bang Theory* is one of the top Indians in American fandom. His name, appropriately, means king.

Rani means queen. *Doctor Who* offers the villainess "The Rani," while Rani Chandra is a child heroine in the spinoff, *The Sarah Jane Adventures.*

Rohan from *The Maze Runner* is named from the Sanskrit "ascending."

Sandeep Parikh plays Sujan/Zaboo on *The Guild.* His name means virtuous light, a shiny choice.

Sanjay means "Victorious." Sanjaya is a significant character in the Hindu epic *Mahabharata.* Onderon king Sanjay Rash features in *The Clone Wars.* There's Sanjay, Apu's brother in *The Simpsons,* Prince Sanjay of Ishkebar from *The Suite Life of Zack and Cody,* and Professor Sanjay Dravid, a scientist from the *Power of Five* series.

Sayagi from the *Ender's Game* series has a name that means sunset. Very sweet.

Subrahmanyan Chandrasekhar was an astrophysicist who discovered the science of black holes. His name, meaning worthy jewel, certainly sparkles.

Sujan Balakrishnan Goldberg is Zaboo on *The Guild.* (He's from mixed heritage, but his name means "a good man.") He's awfully dweeby, but also a nice guy.

Sunita "Suni" Williams of India and the US was an astronaut on several missions. Her name means "well conducted, polite." In Hindu legend, Sunita was the daughter of King Anga of Bengal.

Virlomi from the *Ender's Game* series is a powerful young leader of India, but fails to appear in baby name guides, only *Ender's Game* ones, suggesting it's made up.

Russian/Northern European

Anya see Anne

Dmitri Mendeleev created the periodic table. From Demeter, the name means "earth lover." It's notciably more popular in Russia than Demeter is in Europe.

Domovoi Butler is Artemis Fowl's bodyguard. A domovoi is an eastern European house spirit, and thus a strange choice. His first name may have defined his life nearly as much as the second one.

Ivan Pavlov worked out the conditioned reflex. Another Ivan is Black Widow's go-to-guy in Marvel comics. A respectable Russian and science discoveries name…until you tell the kid his name comes from dog-drool experiments. Four happy babies. See Navi for Ivan spelled backwards.

Ilya comes from the Biblical Elijah, "He is my God." Real life offers Nobel Prize winners Russian physicist Ilya Mikhailovich Frank and Belgian physical chemist Ilya Romanovich Prigogine. There was also Ilya Perfilyev, a Russian explorer.

Russian folk hero Ilya Muromets takes the fiction side, as do characters in Chekhov and Dostoevsky. There's also Ilya Pasternak from the video game *Ace Combat 6: Fires of*

Liberation and Ilya Kuryakin, a main character on *The Man from U.N.C.L.E.* Illyana Nikolievna Rasputina is the X-Man Magik (sister of Colossus).

Katarina see Katherine

Katsa, a variant on Katherine, pure, goes to the warrior heroine of Kristin Cashore's *Graceling.*

Kirjava, Finnish for multi-coloured, is the feline embodiment of a hero's soul in *His Dark Materials.* Meow.

The rugged and roguish Kristoff of *Frozen* shared a name with 32 baby boys recently (Wolfers). See Christopher.

Larissa see Lara

Leonid is a young Russian magician in Rick Riordan's *The Kane Chronicles.* See Leonard.

Nikolai Delphiki is a major character in *Ender's Shadow* and another is Worf's brother on *Star Trek.* See Nicholas.

Olaf, *Frozen*'s lovable snowman, now has 22 baby namesakes, up from only nine the previous year. Now that's a laugh. Count Olaf is also the supervillain of *A Series of Unfortunate Events.*

Pavel Chekhov has a name that's Russian for little. It's the variant on "Paul."

Petra ("stone") appears in *Shingeki no Kyojin* and is a heroine of *Ender's Game.* See Peter.

Sonya shares a name with Red Sonja the barbarian superhero. It's a variant on Sophia, wisdom.

55 baby Svens (the reindeer of *Frozen*) were born right after the film, up from 33 in 2013 (Wolfers). Svens have appeared in *Titanic,* Pixar's *Cars* (voiced by Arnold Schwarzenegger), as a Nintendo *Pokémon*, a *Skyrim* hero, and a manga character. Sven, the Warrior of the North, is the icon of the 319th Air Refueling Wing, Grand Forks Air Force Base, North Dakota.

Svetlana Savitskaya of the Soviet Union was an astronaut on Soyuz T-7/5, Soyuz T-12. The name means "star," with another namesake in a *Resident Evil* movie.

In Neil Gaiman's *The Sandman,* Vassily appears as an old man telling his teenaged granddaughter a tale from "the old country," medieval Russia. This name is from Basil, "royal."

Vera Black is a British psionic cyborg in the DC Universe. The name is Russian for "summer."

Viktualia is the Swedish equivalent of "Delicatessa" and Pippi Longstocking's middle name. I like Delicatessa myself. Yum!

Vlad from the *Ender's Game* series unfortunately shares a name with Vlad Dracula, the original vampire's inspiration. It means "renowned prince" though renowned for what, precisely, is the question. Watch the breastfeeding.

In another *Dracula* reference, the students of *Vampire Academy* attend St. Vladimir's. Vladimir Menshikov is the antagonist of Rick Riordan's *The Throne of Fire,* described as an "evil ice cream man" for his white suits.

Vladimir Ivanovich Vernadsky is a renowned Russian crystallographer, mineralogist, geochemist and geologist who laid out the foundation for the study of geochemistry.

There's also Vladimir Prelog, winner of the Nobel Prize for Chemistry.

Yuri Gagarin was an astronaut on Vostok 1 and the first person in space. While Yuri Lowell is a lead in the Japanese video game *Tales of Vesperia*, Yuri is also a term in manga used for lesbian romance. The name is actually derived from George, "farmer."

Spanish

Adora is the princess who can turn into She-Ra, mightiest supergirl of all. Also, Adora Belle Dearheart is a character in Terry Pratchett's Discworld. She loathes her cutesy name – just a warning. It's a Spanish name, unsurprisingly short for Adoración, adoration.

Angela Del Toro is Marvel superhero White Tiger, while Ángela Ruiz Robles was the pioneer of the electronic book. See Angel

Carmela Rodriguez is Kit's sister in the *Young Wizards* series. A Catholic name, it's the title of the Virgin Mary Our Lady of Carmel. A variant, Carmen, is famous through the opera and Carmen Sandiego. Carmen, Queen of the Underworld, is Ofelia's mother in *Pan's Labyrinth*.

Emilio G. Segrè won the Nobel Prize in Physics, while Emilio Herrera Linares (1879-1967) is the inventor of the original space suit. Emilio ("rival") is a good scientist name with a competitive edge.

See Hector

His name is Inigo Montoya…you killed his father…prepare to die. If you name your child this, everyone will chant this at him day and night. True, it's a real name, Spanish-Castillian for "little love" or Greek for fiery, from several St Ignatiuses. But four sad babies say you shouldn't take the chance.

Jesus Velasquez is a charming brujo and love interest on *True Blood.*

José lends itself to scientists, discoverers, and inventors such as naturalist José de Acosta (1540–1600) and José María Algué, who invented the barocyclometer, the nephoscope, and the microseismograph. José Ignacio Barraquer invented the microkeratome and the cryolathe, and developed surgical procedures of refractive surgery. It's a variant on Biblical Joseph, "may God increase." Certainly, the creativity and brains seem increased here.

Juanita "Nita" Louise Callahan is the heroine of the *Young Wizards* series. Juan is a *Pokémon* character, and there's one in *Starsship Troopers.* In history, Juan Ignacio Cirac Sasturain pioneered quantum computing and quantum information theory. Aeronautical engineer Juan de la Cierva invented the autogyro. These mean "God is gracious."

Julio ("youthful") Cervera Baviera is considered by some to be the actual inventor of the radio.

Luís Ponce de León, the explorer, appears in many novels and adaptations. It means "renowned warrior." There's also Luís Walter Alvarez and Luís Federico Leloir, winners of the Nobel Prize in Physics and Chemistry respectively. See Louis

Manuel Cardona Castro researched superconductivity and the interaction of electromagnetic radiation with a semiconductor material. Manuel Garcia invented the laryngoscope, while Manuel Jalón Corominas invented a two-piece disposable syringe. And, oddly, the mop. Guess someone had to. From Emmanuel, "God is with us."

Maria Jackson is a young hero in *The Sarah Jane Adventures* and Maria Mendoza is a heroine in the YA dystopia *The House of the Scorpion* by Nancy Farmer. Another appears in the video game *Silent Hill 2*. There's Wall Maria, the wall protecting humanity in the anime/ manga *Attack on Titan*. Maria Mitchell was the first female American professional astronomer. It means "bitter" or "wished-for." Second most popular name in Spain.

Miguel is from the Biblical Michael, "who is like God." There's one in Dreamworks' *The Road to El Dorado.* Miguel Servet was the first European to understand pulmonary circulation. Miguel de Cervantes arguably wrote the first novel, *Don Quixote.*

Morena Baccarin plays Inara on *Firefly*. The name is Spanish for brunette, if you can judge the hair color ahead of time with your mutant precognition.

Pedro Duque was an astronaut on two missions. It means rock. I guess he did.

See Raphael

Raul is the romantic hero of *The Phantom of the Opera.* This is a variant on Randolph/Ralph, "wolf counsel."

Rita is Spanish for pearl. Rita Skeeter is the irritating reporter for the *Daily Prophet*, while Rita Farr Dayton is Elasti-Girl. That's one good namesake and one bad one…without much scifi. Of course, Rita Repulse is a disturbing variant in *Mighty Morphin Power Rangers.*

Rodrigo ("famous ruler") López de Segura (1540-1580) was a chess expert and author of the definitive book on the subject, for fanatics of the game. See Roderick

Santiago comes from the Spanish Santo Iago, Saint James. There's one who's a vampire in Anne Rice's *The Vampire Chronicles* and this is vampire Raphael's last name in *The Mortal Instruments.* Santiago Ramón y Cajal (1852–1934) was the father of Neuroscience and a Nobel prize Laureate.

Serafina Pekkala is a witch-heroine of the *Golden Compass* series. It's Spanish/Hebrew for angel, heavenly, or possibly fire. Seems sibilant but tough to spell.

Sirena is Latin/Spanish for mermaid, so the romantic hero of *Pirate of the Caribbean: On Stranger Tides,* names his mermaid love this. Also a heroine on original *Battlestar Galactica.*

Sources

This book includes references to the following (and more as well):

Actors
Authors
Astronauts
Scientists
Alice in Wonderland
Angel
Anime/Manga
Anne Rice
Avatar
Babylon 5
Being Human
The Big Bang Theory
Blake's 7
Buffy the Vampire Slayer
Charmed
SF and F novels
Children's books
The Dark Crystal
DC Comics
Discworld
Disney
Divergent
Doctor Who
Dollhouse
Dragonriders of Pern
Dune
Earthsea
Ender's Game
Eragon
Farscape
Firefly
Game of Thrones
Ghostbusters
The Golden Compass
The Guild
Harry Potter
Hitchhiker's Guide to the Galaxy
The Hunger Games
Inkheart
King Arthur
Labyrinth
Ladyhawke
Lord of the Rings
Lost
The Last Unicorn
Madeline L'Engle
Marvel Comics
Masters of the Universe
The Maze Runner
Mistborn
Mirrormask
Monty Python
Myth and history
Narnia
The Neverending Story
The Nightmare before Christmas
Once Upon a Time

Patrick Rothfuss's *The Kingkiller Chronicle.*
Percy Jackson
Tamora Pierce
Pókemon
Quantum Leap
Rocky Horror
The Sandman
Sherlock
Space Above and Beyond.
Stargate
Star Trek
Star Wars
The Sword of Truth
J.R.R. Tolkien
True Blood
The Vampire Diaries
The Wheel of Time
Wicked
Willow
Wizard of Oz
Patricia C. Wrede
X-Files
X-Men

Additional thanks to:

Appellation Mountain. "Echo, Xander, Zoe: Joss Whedon Baby Names." 8 March 2013. http://appellationmountain.net/echo-xander-zoe-joss-whedon-baby-names.

Campbell, Mike. *Behindthename.com*

Chevalier, Jean and Alain Gheerbrant. *A Dictionary of Symbols.* Trans. John Buchanan-Brown. Oxford: Blackwell, 1994.

Hendricks, Jaclyn. "*Frozen, Hunger Games* inspire 2014's most popular baby names." *The New York Post* 2 Dec 2014. http://nypost.com/2014/12/02/frozen-hunger-games-inspire-2014s-most-popular-baby-names.

Holeman, Heather. "Most Popular *Star Wars* Baby Names." *Kfor* 10 Nov 2015. http://kfor.com/2015/11/10/most-popular-star-wars-baby-names.

Milbrand, Lisa. "Buffy the Vampire Slayer's Influence on Baby Names." *Parents Magazine* 22 May 2013. http://www.parents.com/blogs/in-name-only/2013/05/22/must-read/buffy-the-vampire-slayers-influence-on-baby-names.

MooseRoots. "25 Adorable Halloween-inspired Baby Names." *Tribune Media Wire* 30 Oct 2015. http://kfor.com/2015/10/30/25-adorable-halloween-inspired-baby-names.

Poladian, Charles. "*Game Of Thrones* Baby Names: Arya for Girls and Theon for Boys in Britain." *IBT Pulse* 17 Aug 2015. http://www.ibtimes.com/pulse/game-thrones-baby-names-arya-girls-theon-boys-britain-2057088.

Rosenkrantz, Linda and Pamela Redmond Satran. *Nameberry.com*.

Wolfers, Justin. "After 'Frozen,' a Baby Boomlet of Elsas" *The Upshot* July 2, 2015 http://www.nytimes.com/2015/07/02/upshot/frozen-and-the-rise-of-elsa.html.

About the Author

Valerie Estelle Frankel is the author of many books on pop culture, including *Doctor Who – The What, Where, and How, Sherlock: Every Canon Reference You May Have Missed in BBC's Series 1-3, History, Homages and the Highlands: An Outlander Guide,* and *How Game of Thrones Will End*. Many of her books focus on women's roles in fiction, from her heroine's journey guides *From Girl to Goddess* and *Buffy and the Heroine's Journey* to books like *Women in Game of Thrones* and *The Many Faces of Katniss Everdeen.* Once a lecturer at San Jose State University, she's a frequent speaker at conferences. Come explore her research at www.vefrankel.com.

www.ingramcontent.com/pod-product-compliance
Lightning Source LLC
Chambersburg PA
CBHW031510040426
42445CB00009B/169

9780692587362